Fish

Marine Fish and Freshwater Fish Across the World

Peter Attwell

Published in 2014 by

PEG Publishing

ISBN 978-0-9928368-1-8

A CIP catalogue record of this book is available from the British Library

Cover designed by Dr. Jay Polma

Printed and bound in Great Britain

By Lightning Source UK Ltd, Milton Keynes, UK

Foreword

Fish are some of the most diverse and interesting creatures in the world, but many people know remarkably little about them. Within the pages of this book you will find a wealth of information about these fascinating creatures including their evolutionary history, their anatomy and physiology, even their methods of reproduction.

In reading this book you will have even your most pressing questions about these wonderful animals answered in detail.

Acknowledgements

I would like to extend my sincerest thanks to my friends and family for supporting me in my obsession with fish. Without your patient understanding I could not have finished this book. Thank you.

Fish

Marine Fish and Freshwater Fish Across the World

PEG Publishing

Table of Contents

Introduction

Fish can be found in nearly every aquatic environment on the planet from the depths of the largest sea to the shallows of the rice paddies in Thailand. There are an estimated 32,000 different species of fish in existence today and these creatures exhibit more diversity among species than any other type of animal. Having evolved over a period of more than 500 million years, fish are an incredibly interesting and unique group of animals to study.

In this book you will find a wealth of information about fish from their evolutionary history to their modern appearances and behaviours. Here you will read the story of how a species as complex and beautiful as the Lionfish evolved from something as plain and simple as the jawless Agnathans. You will also receive insight into the plight of modern fishes and their struggle to survive the destruction of their habitats and other conservation concerns.

You will find that this book provides a comprehensive overview of fishes, both ancient and modern. Topics to be covered include everything from anatomy and physiology to reproduction and conservation. By the time you finish this book you will find the answers to many of your most pressing questions about fish, the finned wonders of our world.

Chapter One: History of Fish

As you may already know, fish are among the first vertebrates that existed on the planet and they remain some of the oldest creatures in existence. The evolutionary history of fish is long and complex, but it is definitely worth studying. In this chapter you will learn the basics about the evolutionary history of fish dating from 500 million years ago to today. As you will soon see, many of the first fish that evolved are still in existence today in one form or another. You may be surprised to learn that you might have even seen a "living fossil" yourself.

1) Evolution of Fish

Fish have existed on the earth for roughly 500 million years and, during that time, they have evolved into more than 30,000 different species. Throughout their long history, fish have adapted to survive and thrive in nearly every aquatic habitat on the planet – even in the depths of the ocean where the light of the sun cannot penetrate. Not only are fish incredibly interesting and diverse creatures, but they are also known to be a stepping stone in the evolutionary history of land-walking vertebrates.

In order to understand the evolutionary history of fish, you must begin by learning about some of the first fish. Fish are what are known as "true chordates" – chordates are animals that have a dorsally situated central nervous system, gill clefts and a notochord in some stage of development. A notochord is defined as a rod that extends the length of the body, for example, a spine – that provides structure and support during movement. Some other physical characteristics shared by chordates include:

- Bilateral symmetry in the body.
- A segmented body.
- A single nerve cord positioned dorsal to the gut.
- A tail projecting beyond the anus (in any stage of development).
- A central nervous system.
- An endoskeleton – either bony or cartilaginous.
- Pharyngeal pouches in some stage of development.
- A closed blood system with ventral heart as well as ventral and dorsal blood vessels.
- A complete and functional digestive system.

The earliest vertebrate fossil belonged to the Upper Cambrian fossil Anaspis and it is more than 500 million years old. Though the fossil itself is largely fragmented, the animal to which it belongs is thought to be a type of jawless, armored fish. The period of time between about 443 and 417 million years ago is known as the Silurian period and it was during this period of time that jawless fish first began to diversify. It was not until the Devonian period, however, that any true variety was achieved.

The Devonian period lasted for roughly 63 years, beginning about 417 million years ago and ending with the start of the Carboniferous period 354 million years ago. This period of time is often referred to as the "Age of Fishes" because it was during this time that several major lineages of fish began. During the Devonian period, the global climate was warm and sea levels were high – both of these factors contributed to an ideal environment for evolution. Throughout this period, fish developed adaptations specific to their aquatic niche which eventually led to adaptations in the first land animals, amphibians.

2) Early Species of Fish

The first vertebrates, and also the first fish, were the Agnathans. These fish were jawless, possessing rounded mouth parts that were used for filter feeding or sucking. This type of mouth is still found on modern fish such as lampreys and hagfish. The Agnathans were largely bottom-feeding fish and their bodies were heavily armored to protect them from predators. With the exception of the two species already mentioned, most Agnathans are currently extinct.

The next group of fish to evolve were jawed fish (Acanthodians) and they evolved only once – as opposed to evolving several times through parallel evolution in multiple species. The gill arches found in Agnathans evolved into jaws as they fused to the skull, giving these fish the ability to consume a much wider variety of foods. This evolution is also what allowed fish to diverge from being passive filter feeders into becoming active predators in their aquatic environments which led to other morphological adaptations.

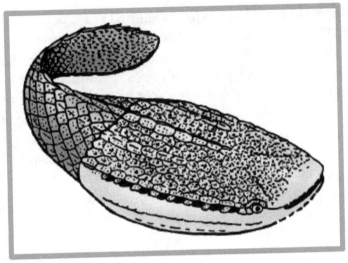

1: Astraspis desiderata

As the mouths of fish evolved to expand the foods fish could ingest, so did their bodies adapt to become better predators. Muscle density decreased as fish led more active lives and their body armor decreased with their need for protection. Over time, fish became more agile and streamlined to enhance their movement through the water in seeking and catching prey.

Coexisting with the Acnathodians during the Silurian period were a group of heavily armored fish called Placoderms. These fish dominated the Devonian period and, though they began small, they eventually came to be very large – up to 35 feet (10.6 meters) long. What made these fish unique was the presence of a movable joint between the head and body which enabled the head to rock backward, opening the jaw very wide. The largest Placoderm living during the Devonian period was the Dunkleosteus, a species which is now extinct.

Though Placoderms are all extinct, some fish which evolved during the same period continue to exist. These fish are members of the class Chondritchthyes which includes sharks, skates and rays and they are commonly referred to as cartilaginous fish. Cartilaginous fish do not have any bone – rather, they possess cartilage and calcified cartilage for internal support. Though this type of skeleton is delicate, it is also light which enabled this group of fishes to become quick and agile predators.

In addition to their flexible skeletons, Chondritchthyes fish also developed two different types of jaws. Sharks have powerful jaws made for crushing and biting while skates and rays have rasping jaws designed for bottom-feeding. Modern sharks are often referred to as "living fossils" since they have not undergone a great deal of evolution for hundreds of millions of years. There are many species of shark, however, which once existed that are no longer living. Some sharks that existed during the Late Paleozoic period, for example, possessed coils of serrated teeth and could grow up to 46 feet (14 meters) long which is more than double the length of the Great White shark.

As Placoderms and sharks began to recede in dominance during the mid to late Devonian period, another group of fishes began to evolve – bony fish. This group of fish is incredibly diverse but all bony fish share one very important characteristic – a swim bladder. A swim bladder is an internal organ thought to have evolved from lungs which enables the fish to float at any water level.

There are three major groups of bony fish: ray-fin fish, lungfish and lobed-fin fish. Ray-fin fish can be found in both fresh and saltwater and they are some of the most common bony fish still alive today such as bass, tuna and salmon. Lungfish are all freshwater fish and they are bottom-feeders. This group of fish receives its name from the fact that they can get up to 90 per cent of their oxygen from the air. Lobed-fin fish were thought to be extinct until a live specimen of Coelacanth was discovered in the 1930s. These fish exhibit walking-like movements with their fins and they are thought to be an ancestor of the first land-walking vertebrates.

3) Oldest Living Fish

As was mentioned in the previous section, the Coelacanth was thought to be extinct until a live specimen was found during the 1930s. These fish have the oldest known living lineage of all fish, being more closely related to lungfish and reptiles than to modern ray-finned fishes that are common today. The name Coelacanth is actually derived from the order name of the fish – Coelacanthiformes – and it is shared with only two species, the West Indian Ocean Coelacanth (*Latimeria chalumnae*) and the Indonesian Coelacanth (*Latimeria menadoensis*).

2: *Preserved specimen of Latimeria chalumnae*

The first living specimen of Coelacanth was a *Latimeria chalumnae* found off the east coast of South Africa in 1938. The fish was found living in the Chalumna River (now known as Tyolomnqa) by museum curator Marjorie Courtenay-Latimer when examining the catch of a local angler named Captain Hendrick Hoosen. A living specimen of *Latimeria menadoensis* was not discovered until 1998 by Mark V. Erdmann and it was described a year later by Pouyaud et al. in Manado, Indonesia.

The Coelacanth is a large lobe-finned fish but it has several unique characteristics which distinguish it from other lobe-finned fishes. First, the Coelacanth possesses a three-lobed caudal fin (also known as a trilobate fin) as well as a secondary tail. These fish have thick armor all over their bodies to serve as protection. Internally, the Coelacanth has a hinged joint inside its head which allows it to open its jaw very wide. Another unique characteristic of these fish is that they still possess a hollow notochord rather than a vertebral column like many modern vertebrates. In fact, the name Coelacanth comes from the Latin for "hollow spine."

Chapter Two: All About Fish

Having read a little about the evolutionary history of fish, it should be clear to you that fish are very unique creatures. These creatures have evolved and adapted over hundreds of millions of years to be the masters of their aquatic domains in every way possible. If you look at the body of a fish, you can see that it is specifically designed to travel quickly through water and many species have specific adaptations to make them more efficient predators. In this chapter you will read about the physical characteristics of fish that make them so unique and interesting. Here you will find an overview of the anatomy and physiology of fish including an explanation of their sensory systems and their methods of locomotion.

1) Anatomy and Physiology

The anatomy of fish involves the use of terms like "dorsal" and "lateral" with which you may not be familiar. Consult the picture below for an explanation of the anatomical directions used in describing fish anatomy:

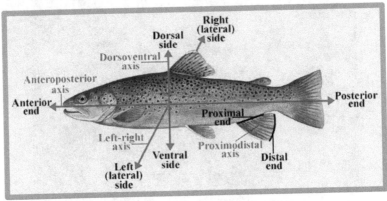

3: Anatomical directions and axes of fish

The body of a fish may take one of three forms: fusiform, filiform or vermiform. A fusiform body is streamlined from nose to tail and it is a body plan often seen in fast-moving fish. A filiform body is long and eel-like while a vermiform body is worm-shaped. A fish's body may also be described as being laterally compressed (thin) or laterally depressed (flat) like flatfish and stingrays.

Fish are vertebrates which means that they have a skeletal system. There are, however, two different types of skeletons in fish: endoskeleton and exoskeleton. An endoskeleton is an internal structure formed from bones that serves to support and protect the body and organs. An exoskeleton is a stable outer shell, often made of cartilage or scales. An example of fish having an exoskeleton are the armored, jawless fishes that lived during the Paleozoic period.

As vertebrates, all fish have a body plan similar among all chordates – they have a notochord or vertebral column (the stiff rod running along the length of the body) with a spinal cord above and the gastrointestinal tract running below. The mouth of a fish is located on the anterior end of the animal and the anus near the posterior end. The body of the fish continues past the anus, however, in a tail that contains only vertebrae, cartilage and scales. Different species of fish exhibit a different number and arrangement of fins, but all possess a caudal fin (tail).

a) External Anatomy

Though the shape, size and placement of various characteristics may vary from one species to another, most fish have similar external anatomy. Below you will find a list of the external anatomical features found on most species of fish:

Fins – the most obvious external appendages on a fish are its fins. The fins of a fish are composed of stiff rays or spines covered by skin. In some species, the fins are bony and unjointed while others have soft, separated fins.

There are six different types of fin, each with its own unique function:

- **Dorsal Fin** – located along the back of the fish, the dorsal fin serves to keep the fish stable while swimming; most species have one dorsal fin, but it is possible to have two or three.

- **Ventral Fin** – also known as the pelvic fins, the ventral fins are located in pairs on the underside of the fish below the pectoral fins; these fins help the fish to make sharp turns or stops and they also help the fish move up and down in the water.

- **Caudal Fin** – also known as the tail; located on the posterior end of the fish and used to aid in locomotion; this fin is typically fan-shaped though some species exhibit a caudal fin that is rounded, truncated, forked or continuous.

- **Anal Fin** – the anal fin is located along the ventral surface of the fish just behind the anus; used for stability while swimming

- **Pectoral Fin** – a pair of pectoral fins is located (one on each side) of the body behind the operculum; these fins aid in sideways locomotion and help some species to maintain depth in the water.

- **Adipose Fin** – this fin is soft and fleshy, located along the back just behind the dorsal fin and forward of the caudal fin; not all fish families have an adipose fin but, for those that do, it is thought to serve a sensory purpose in touch and hearing.

Skin – the skin of a fish is divided into two layers: the epidermis and the dermis. The epidermis is the outer layer of skin and it is composed of epithelial cells which are constantly shed and replaced by new cells. These cells are layered on top of each other, interspersed with slime cells that produce a mucus that forms a protective coating over the skin. The dermis is the layer of skin beneath the epidermis and it is the layer from which the scales of the fish grow. This layer of skin is composed of blood vessels, fibroblasts and collagen.

Scales – the scales of a fish grow from the dermis and are covered by a layer of epithelial cells. There are two different types of scales: one in which the edges are smooth and one in which the edges are serrated. Some species of fish, like armored catfish, have bony plates covering their bodies rather than scales. A fish's scales serve as a coat of flexible armor, protecting the body of the fish.

Pigment Cells – the pigment cells in a fish's skin and scales are what give the fish its colour. Pigment cells are named for the colour of the pigment they contain and the colour of the cells may change. The scientific name for the pigment-containing cells which reflect light to produce colour is 'chromatophore'.

There are six different subclasses of chromatophore:

- Xanthophore (yellow)
- Erythrophore (red)
- Leucophore (white)
- Melanophore (black/brown)
- Cyanophore (blue)
- Iridophore (reflective/iridescent)

Gills – the gills are the means through which fish breathe underwater and they are located on either side of the fish's body, typically behind the eyes. The gills themselves are composed of blood vessels covered by a thin layer of epithelial cells which facilitate the process of gas exchange. These gills are mounted on four gill arches, the tissue which lies between five slit-like openings on either side of the fish's body.

Lateral Line – this part of the fish is often referred to as the "sixth sense" of the fish because it provides extra sensory information. The lateral line of a fish is comprised of numerous modified scales in which a hair cell sits in a pore or pit. These pores are interconnected through a system of canals beneath the skin which contain nerve fibers and other sensory cells which runs from the gills to the tail. Not only does the lateral line enhance the touch and hearing of fish, but it can also help some species to detect electrical currents in the water.

b) Internal Anatomy

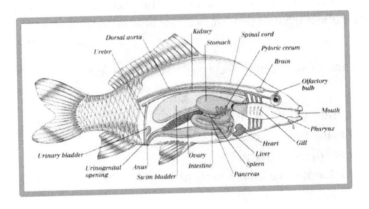

The internal anatomy of fish, like all other vertebrates, consists of a number of different organs. Below you will find an explanation of the location and function of each of these vital organs:

Heart – the heart of a fish has two chambers consisting of an atrium and a ventricle. The atrium of the heart serves to receive blood and the ventricle pumps it throughout the body. In some cases, the entry and exit compartments of the heart are referred to as "chambers" as well so it is not uncommon to see the heart of a fish labeled four-chambered. The atrium and the ventricle are the only two "true" chambers, however – the others are considered accessory.

Liver – the liver is a vital organ found in all types of fish. This organ serves a number of essential functions including protein synthesis, detoxification and the production of certain biochemical needed for digestion.

Kidneys – a fish has two kidneys, both narrow and elongated that take up a significant portion of the trunk of the body. These organs contain groups of nephrons which serve to regulate the concentration of water and sodium in the blood. The kidneys help to filter the blood, excreting waste products through urine.

Intestines – all fish have intestines consisting of two segments: the large and the small intestines. Bony fish have relatively short intestines, measuring only one and a half times the body length of the fish. Certain non-teleost fish like sharks and lungfish have no small intestine – rather, the intestines form a sort of spiral, connecting the stomach directly to the rectum.

Pyloric Caeca – this particular organ is a type of pouch positioned at the beginning of the large intestine. The pyloric caeca receives fecal matter and connects to the colon in the large intestine to pass it along through the body for excretion.

Stomach – the position of the stomach is fairly constant among most species of fish. Generally, the esophagus and duodenum open to the stomach and it curves back to the left in order to meet the pyloric sphincter. Certain species of fish, however, such as lampreys, hagfishes and lungfishes have no stomach at all. Rather, the esophagus opens right into the intestine.

Spleen – the spleen is a non-vital organ but it is found in almost all vertebrate species. This organ looks similar to a lymph node and it serves to filter the blood, aiding the immune system and the production of red blood cells.

Swim Bladder – also referred to as the gas bladder, the swim bladder helps fish to retain their buoyancy. With this organ, fish are able to ascend or descend through the water without having to expend any energy on swimming. Only bony fishes possess a swim bladder and, in some more primitive species, it doubles as a lung.

Reproductive Organs – the reproductive organs of fish are called gonads and, in most species, they appear in pairs of similar size. Male fishes possess two testes which produce and release sperm (often called milt) during mating. Female fish possess ovaries which may contain hundreds of millions of eggs.

Weberian Apparatus – this structure is something that some fish have developed to help them hear more clearly. The Weberian Apparatus is found in fishes belonging to the superorder Ostariophysi and it works in conjunction with the swim bladder. Fish having this modification possess a set of bones called Weberian ossicles which connect the swim bladder to the auditory system, thus allowing the transmission of vibrations from the water around the fish into the inner ear.

Labyrinth – a lung-like organ found in certain freshwater fish belonging to the suborder Anabantoidei (also known as anabantids of labyrinth fish). This organ allows fish to breathe oxygen directly from the air at the surface of the water, rather than filtering it through their gills. Having a labyrinth allows fish to survive for short periods of time out of water – this is a particularly useful adaptation seen in Betta fish (Siamese Fighting Fish). These fish live in shallow puddles and rice paddies and, when their puddles dry up, must seek new water sources – a labyrinth allows them to survive for short periods of time out of the water as they seek a new environment.

c) Physiology of Fish

Central Nervous System – compared to other vertebrates, the brain of a fish is very small relative to its body size. Some species, however – such as sharks – have very large brains. The brain of a fish is divided into different regions, or lobes. At the front of the brain are the olfactory lobes – this structure receives and processes signals to give the fish its sense of smell. The next section is the diencephalon which regulates hormones and homeostasis.

The midbrain, also called the mesencephalon, houses two optic lobes – these are the structures which give the fish sight. Behind the midbrain is the hindbrain, the metencephalon, which serves to regulate balance and swimming. The cerebellum is the largest structure in the brain. Behind the cerebellum is the brain stem (or myelencephalon) which helps to control muscles and organs as well as respiration and osmoregulation.

Immune System – the immune systems of fish vary depending on the species. In jawless fish, for example, lymphoid organs are not present. Jawless fish like hagfish and lampreys rely instead on lymphoid tissue within their other organs to produce and regulate immune cells. Cartilaginous fish like rays and sharks, on the other hand, have much more advanced immune systems. These fish have three specialised organs which make up the immune system: the epigonal organs, the Leydig's organ and a spiral valve.

The epigonal organ surrounds the gonads and the Leydig's organ is located within the esophageal wall. The spiral valve is found in the intestine. Each of these organs contains immune cells which work in conjunction with the spleen and thymus to regulate immune function. Bony fishes possess immune tissues in many parts of the body including the kidney, thymus, spleen, gills, gut and gonads. Some species even have lymphatic systems similar to those found in mammals.

Digestive System – the digestive system of fish functions in a similar manner to that of all other vertebrates. The jaws allows for the ingestion of food before it is broken down and passed through the esophagus into the stomach. In the stomach, food is further digested by digestive enzymes which break down the food and help the body to absorb the nutrients it contains. The food then moves through the digestive tract, aided by enzymes and chemicals produced by the liver and pancreas, and the process of digestion is completed in the intestines.

Osmoregulation – the figure above depicts the process of osmoregulation which is defined as the regulation of the osmotic pressure in an organism's fluids to maintain homeostasis. This is the system that keeps the fluids in a fish's body from becoming either too concentrated or too diluted in terms of ionic content. Osmoregulation differs slightly between saltwater and freshwater fish because saltwater has a high concentration of sodium and other ions. Saltwater fish are referred to as "osmoconformers" because they match the osmolarity of their bodies to that of their environment. Osmoregulators, like freshwater fish, regulate their osmolarity to remain constant.

Thermoregulation – fish are ectothermic organisms which means that their body temperature is regulated by the temperature of their surrounding environment. Different species of fish exhibit various methods of thermoregulation. Sharks, for example, are poikilothermic which means that their internal body temperature is the same as that of their environment. Certain species of bony fish, however, are homeothermic – they can maintain an elevated body temperature different from that of their environment.

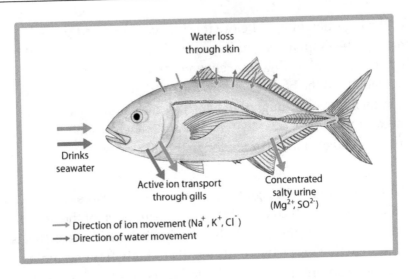

Muscular System – you will learn more about fish locomotion later in this chapter but, essentially, fish move by alternately contracting paired muscles on either side of the body. As the fish contracts these paired muscles, S-shaped curves move along the length of the body and, when the curve reaches the caudal fin, a backward force is applied against the water to create forward motion. The fins of a fish serve to increase the surface area of the tail, increasing the speed of the fish's movement and providing a means of steering through the water.

Most fish have white flesh, but the muscle tissue of some species may be dark pink or even red (ex: salmon). What makes red muscle tissue red is the presence of myoglobin, an oxygen-binding molecule, in the muscle. The presence of myoglobin in the tissue not only changes the colour of the muscle, but also enables quicker energy delivery to the muscle of the fish. White muscle tissue, on the other hand, does not require oxygen and it is only useful for short bursts of speed. Red muscle tissue is designed for sustained activity such as cruising along at a low speed.

Respiratory System – as you already know, fish breathe by absorbing oxygen from the water around them using their gills. The gills are simply tissues made of threadlike filaments that facilitate ion and water transfer as well as gas exchange. In order to breathe, fish pull water into their mouths and pump it over the gills – the gills absorb the oxygen from the water and push it back out of the body through the openings on the side of the throat (pharynx).

2) Sensory Systems

The sensory systems of fish are very similar to that of humans and other vertebrates. Like a human, a fish has five different senses: sight, smell, touch, taste and hearing. One might also argue that the lateral line of a fish provides a sixth sense. Below you will find an explanation of each of these senses as they apply to fish:

a) Sight

A fish's eyes are very similar to that of a human's they contain both rods and cones as well as the same three chemicals that enable humans to see on a spectrum of seven colours. What makes the eyes of fish unique, however, is a fourth chemical which allows them to see in the ultraviolet range of light. Another feature of a fish's eye is a mirror-like layer at the back of the eye that reflects light, causing it to pass through the eye twice (raccoons and other nocturnal animals have this same feature).

Though forward-pointing eyes are typically the mark of a predator, all types of fish have eyes on either side of their head, even predatory species. This being the case, a fish can see two different images at the same time. Though this feature allows a fish to see more of its environment at once, the two-dimensionality of its vision makes it difficult for the fish to judge distances. Despite this, some fish like the trout have remarkably strong vision. A study performed by Tom Hrabik at the University of Minnesota Duluth revealed that young trout were very adept at seeing their prey in low levels of light. Most fish, however, do not rely on sight as their primary sense.

b) Smell

The sense of smell is perhaps the most highly developed sense in fish and it is typically used more often than sight in the detection of food. Because fish live underwater, it may seem strange that they have a sense of smell – but you have to remember that fish breathe through their gills, not through their nose like a human would. Rather, the nose is used to detect chemical traces in the water. Some fish, like salmon, have olfactory senses stronger even than a human's.

A study conducted by Arthur Hasler revealed that scent plays a key role in helping adult salmon to find their home streams for spawning. These salmon are able to follow scent trails remembered from years past to locate the stream year after year. The olfactory sense of salmon is so strong that they are able to detect the odor of certain bile acids at a concentration of less than a thimble-full in over a billion gallons of water. Similarly, a shark's nose is able to detect blood at a concentration as little as one part per million.

c) Touch

Though fish do not have fingers or hands with which to feel things, they still have very sensitive skin. In fact, fish have a very elevated tactile sense through the lateral line. The lateral line in fish is composed of numerous neuromasts which are essentially hair cells at the bottom of a pit that function as sensory cells. When moved, these cells convert mechanical energy into electrical energy to enhance the fish's senses of touch and even hearing. These cells allow fish to sense even the most subtle changes in water pressure around them.

Some fish (such as sharks and catfish) also have the ability to detect electrical currents in the water, even currents as weak as a millivolt. Certain species of fish are even able to product their own electric current which they can use in communication and navigation within groups. Of all animals on earth, sharks have the most well developed electrical sensitivity, they can detect prey hidden in the sand using the electric field the prey produces. Electric field proximity sensing is also used by catfish to help them navigate through murky waters. This type of sensing is so advanced that it can detect the shape, size, distance and velocity of objects in their environment.

d) Taste

Like humans, fish have tactile nerve endings in their mouths but also on their bodies and fins. Additionally, most species of fish are able to taste through their skin and lips. An interesting example of this concept is a behaviour exhibited by sharks – they can sometimes be seen rubbing their bodies across potential prey to determine whether or not it is really a source of food. Catfish have the nickname "swimming tongues" because they have taste buds all over their bodies.

For many fish, the sense of taste triggers a reflexive snapping behaviour. According to Peter Sorensen of the Department of Fisheries, trout see their prey first and then they smell it. When they taste the prey, a snapping reflex it automatically triggered. It is common opinion among researchers that fish are able to taste their food long before it even enters their mouth.

e) Hearing

Though a fish's sense of hearing is not particularly well developed, sound travels about five times faster in water than it does in air. A fish may not have external ears in the form you are used to seeing them, but they are still able to make and detect sound. The ears of a fish are called otoliths, though many fish can also sense sound through the lateral line and some through their swim bladders. Carp and herring are known to have particularly well developed senses of hearing.

3) Locomotion

If someone were to ask you how fish move, you would undoubtedly reply that they swim. The real answer, however, is a little more complex, swimming involves the contraction of multiple muscle and the coordination of fins to steer through the water. In order to truly understand fish, you must learn the basics of their locomotion.

One of the essential characteristics fish have that enables them to move as they do is their flexible body plan. Most species of fish have streamlined bodies that enable them to move quickly through the water with very little drag, they are able to make minute adjustments for water currents to increase their speed and to reduce their energy output. The slime coating produced by the fish's body also helps to reduce friction in the water by as much as 65 per cent.

a) Basics of Fish Movement

Having already read about the external anatomy of fish, you already know that the caudal fin (tail) is used primarily for propulsion and the remaining fins for balance and control. While the tail is the most powerful fin, capable of producing quick bursts of speed, most fish are also capable of achieving small but direct movements using only their dorsal, pelvic and pectoral fins. Some species are even able to create undulating movements with their fins to provide a slow but steady forward motion.

In addition to using their fins, most fish also incorporate sinuous body movements to swim. This movement is created by alternately contracting paired muscles on either side of the spinal column to produce a wave-like body motion. As a result of this motion, the tail moves side to side which creates thrust to propel the fish forward. Some species of fish have an elongated body, however, and the entire rear section of the body acts as the caudal fin or tail.

Fish can be divided into three categories by the type of motion they utilise in swimming: anguilliform, ostraciform and carangiform. Anguilliform swimmers are typically those that have an elongated body (like eels, lampreys and lungfish) which create a deep body wave in swimming. Ostraciform swimmers like boxfish and trunkfish are those that actively use the caudal fin for propulsion but leave the rest of the body steady. Carangiform swimmers like tuna are those that flex the body and use the caudal fin, creating an S-like body shape as they swim.

b) Maximum Swimming Speed

Some fish are simply built for speed while others are designed to cruise along on the ocean currents at a slow and steady pace. The speed a fish is capable of reaching depends on its body size and shape. Fish that have less streamlined bodies, for example, may have a lower top speed than fish with more dynamic body shapes. The formula for determining the top swimming speed a fish can achieve is as follows:

$$V = \tfrac{1}{4}\,[L(3f\text{-}4)]$$

V = velocity in meters per second

L = length of the fish in meters

f = frequency of tail beats per second

One of the fastest-swimming fish is the salmon, capable of achieving speeds up to 22.5 kph (14 mph). In comparison, a pike can achieve a top speed around 7kph and a goldfish about 4.8 kph. Remember, however, that the top speed of a fish is relative to its size – a 30 cm (12 inch) Sea Trout can achieve a speed nearing 11 kph (7 mph) but a 20 cm (7.8 inch) Sea Trout may be able to swim only 8 kph (5.4 mph).

You have probably heard of "flying fish" and you may be curious as to how they achieve flight. In reality, flying fish do not achieve what scientists call "powered flight" – rather, they gain momentum in the water and then glide through the air. There are four different families of fish which exhibit this type of locomotion: Belonidae, Dactylopteridae, Exocoetidae and Hemirhamphidae. All of these fish are marine species which have enlarged pectoral fins that are folded against the body while swimming and then opened after the fish leaps from the water.

Flying Fish taking off

Flying fish are able to leap up to 1 meter (3 ft.) out of the water and can travel as fast as 30 kph (20 mph) for hundreds of meters. To prepare for flight, the flying fish will beat its tail rapidly in the water (up to 50 times per second) to increase their speed. This speed pushes the fish's body up out of the water where it unfolds the pectoral fins and glides for 5 to 10 seconds. With proper speed and height, a flying fish can glide for more than 40 seconds.

4) Fish Facts for Kids

Fish are fascinating creatures and they are incredibly popular among children. Much of the information in this book is detailed and complex in nature which may not be ideal for younger children to read and understand. Below you will find a list of fun and interesting fish facts gathered particularly with children in mind:

- Fish are vertebrates (which means they have a spine or backbone) that live in the water.

- There are over 30,000 different species of fish divided into hundreds of different groups.

- Fish can be found living in almost every type of aquatic habitat on the earth.

- Some fish can survive in temperatures below freezing (32°F/0°C) due to anti-freeze chemicals in their blood.

- All fish are cold-blooded creatures which means that their body temperature is affected by the environment around them.

- Fish have been in existence for over 500 million years.

- Some fish can swim very fast – up to 43 miles per hour (70 kilometers per hour).

- Fish have bodies covered in scales which are coated with slime to help them move quickly through the water.

- Different types of fish perform different roles in their environment – some are predators, some are scavenger and some area cleaners.

- Fish breathe underwater using specialised organs called gills which are located on either side of the fish's head.

- The lifespan of fish varies greatly depending on the species – some live only a few weeks while others can live 50 years or more.

- The oldest living species of fish is the Coelacanth.

- The bodies of fish are streamlined which help them to move throughout the water with ease.

Chapter Three: Fish Behaviour

Given that there are thousands of different species of fish on the planet, it should come as no surprise to you that these animals exhibit widely differing behaviours. Some species of fish are very calm and peaceful, tending to live and travel in large groups, while others are highly aggressive and independent. The mating behaviours of fish are also very unique and, depending on the species, can be quite complex. In this chapter you will learn about the basics of fish behaviour including courting/mating behaviours, reproductive methods and other types of behaviour as well. You will also receive a list of fun and interesting fish behaviour facts.

1) Reproduction

The process through which fish eggs are released and fertilised is typically referred to as "spawning." Different species of fish exhibit different types of spawning behaviour and some species do not spawn at all, rather, they give birth to live young. In this section you will learn the basics about different types of fish reproduction.

a) **Types of Reproduction**

Egg Layers – most species of fish are egg layers which means that the female produces eggs and the male fertilises them after they have left the female's body. Different species of egg-laying fish exhibit different egg-laying behaviours. Some, for example, scatter their eggs over a wide area while others deposit them on a flat rock or plant. Some species of egg-layers guard their nests fiercely and even raise their young while others are more likely to eat their own eggs than protect them.

Livebearers – in contrast to fish that lay eggs, livebearers (as suggested by their name) give birth to live young. Some of the most common species of livebearer include mollies, guppies, platies and swordtails. There are two different types of livebearer fish: ovoviviparous and viviparous. Ovoviviparous fish retain the eggs inside the body of the female, but they develop independently without receiving a supply of nutrients from the female's body. Viviparous fish, on the other hand, provide nutrients to the eggs through the blood supply of the female (similar to the placenta in mammals).

Mouth Brooders – a mouth-brooding fish is something of a cross between an egg layer and a livebearer. Cichlids are the most common example of mouth-brooding species, though not all cichlids are mouth-brooders. In these species the female (though it is sometimes the male) gathers the eggs in her mouth to protect them during development. In some species, the male will fertilise the eggs as they are released while, in others, the eggs are fertilised after the female has gathered them. This type of brooding is considered analogous to ovoviviparity because the eggs do not receive any nutrients from the parent. Once the eggs have hatched and the fry (baby fish) have developed, the female releases them into the environment.

b) Courting and Mating Behaviours

Some species of fish (like guppies) are incredibly prolific breeders – they breed easily and often. For other fish, however, breeding is a long and complex process filled with specific behaviours and protocols that must be followed. In most species, the male of the species is larger and more colourful which plays into courting behaviour – he may make displays to attract the female's attention and to secure her interest for himself, fighting off other males. Females, on the other hand, tend to be less colourful in most species.

To initiate courting behaviour, the male of the species will often nudge the female or chase her around. Once the male catches the female, he may drape or wrap himself around the female's body. As the female releases her store of eggs, the male will release his sperm (milt), fertilising them as they are released. In livebearing species of fish, fertilisation is internal and the young are not released until they are fulls formed.

c) Parental Care by Fish

Not all fish exhibit any level of parental care but some are extremely attentive parents. Cichlids, for example, exhibit the highest level of parental care among almost all fishes, often raising their young to adulthood. In cases where parental care is present, you may be interested to learn that the male parent is typically the care-giver. In egg-laying species of fish, the male is usually responsible for preparing a nest or clearing a spawning site. The male will then guide the female to the site for spawning or gather the eggs after their release and relocate them to the nest.

Once the eggs have been placed in the nest, the male will stand guard over them, protecting them from other fish. In some cases, the male and female will alternate care of the eggs until and after they hatch. Most fish that exhibit this type of bi-parental care are monogamous, meaning that they stay together for one or more spawnings. Once the eggs have hatched, the parents will often continue to care for the fry as they grow. In some cases (such as discus fish) the fry will actually feed on mucosal secretions from the bodies of the parent fish.

2) Other Behaviours

While courting and mating behaviours of fish are incredibly

complex and unique, they are not the only interesting behaviours fish exhibit. In addition to mating behaviours, fish also exhibit schooling behaviour, territoriality and aggression as well as some innovative defence and camouflage techniques. In this section you will learn the basics about these fish behaviours.

a) Schooling and Shoaling

Schooling is an incredibly prevalent behaviour among fish, it is estimated that about 80 per cent of fish species exhibit schooling behaviour at some point during their life cycles. This type of behaviour serves as protection for fish (particularly smaller species) and also impacts their ability to reproduce in sufficient numbers. It was Aristotle who first noticed schooling behaviour in fish over 2,400 years ago and, since then, it has been a popular subject of scientific and ecological study.

There are many benefits for schooling behaviour in fish. One of the simplest advantages is that it helps fish to swim more effectively. As you already know, the bodies of fish produce a slime coating which helps to reduce their friction as they travel through the water. Each fish, as it moves its fin and tails, produces its own mini whirlpool – one fish can use the current produced by another fish in the school to further reduce its own friction.

Perhaps the most important advantage schooling behaviour provides, however, is in protection from predators this is based on the concept of "safety in numbers." Small fish that swim close together can give a predator the impression that it is actually one very large fish, thus frightening it off. There is also the factor that a single predator cannot catch and eat all of the fish in the school at once, thus giving the other fish a chance to escape. Schooling fish have the unique ability to sense even the slightest change of speed or direction in the fish around them so they can easily confuse predators by changing the configuration of the group.

b) Aggression and Territoriality

Scientists generally divide competitive behaviour into two categories: exploitative competition and interference competition. Exploitative competition involves one animal out-competing the others in speed or strength, generally for food and mates. Interference competition, however, involves fighting to achieve the best rights for food and mates. Aggression plays a key role in both forms of competition, particularly among fish, in establishing some level of dominance hierarchy.

Though not all fish can be considered "aggressive" by nature, most species will compete for food and will fight fish that they perceive as a threat to their territory. Aggressive behaviour becomes particularly common during mating seasons and when multiple males of the same species occupy the same territory. Some of the most common aggressive behaviours exhibited by fish include: chasing, nipping fins and body ramming. The fish that wins the most fights typically becomes the "alpha" male and has access to the best food and the most suitable mates while the others are relegated to less suitable environments.

c) Defence and Camouflage

Schooling is one of the most common defensive behaviours that fish exhibit, but certain species have developed other adaptations as well. Flatfish, for example, have bodies perfectly designed to lay flat against the riverbed or ocean bottom where they blend in with their environment and when their prey approaches, the fish is able to strike quickly before the prey even knows what is happening. This type of behaviour may also be seen in other species that have developed unique camouflage patterns or colours to blend with a particular environment.

d) Interesting Fish Behaviour Facts

1. Certain species of fish become more active at certain times of the day, for example, bony fishes tend to be most active at dawn and dusk.

2. Many species of fish are capable of producing sound – it is often used in conjunction with reproductive or territorial behaviour.

3. Some species of fish form symbiotic relationships with other species, for example, remoras attach themselves to sharks, feeding on scraps and protecting the shark from parasites.

4. Many species of fish exhibit some level of social organisation built around a dominant male.

5. Fish do sleep, but not in the way we are used to, they do not have eyelids to close but they do go through periods of reduced physical and metabolic activity.

6. The Oscar fish (a type of cichlid) has been known to exhibit dog-like behaviour, begging for food and learning to recognise its owner.

7. Some of the smallest fish can be the most aggressive in defending their territory, for example, the damselfish (family Pomacentridae).

8. Fish generally do not attack humans, but barracudas have been known to confuse shiny objects carried by divers with the scales of their prey.

Chapter Four: Habitats

Fish can be found in nearly every body of water on earth. Over hundreds of millions of years, different species of fish have evolved and adapted to their particular environments in some unique and amazing ways. Some fish, for example, have anti-freeze chemicals in their blood enabling them to live in sub-zero temperatures. Other species have adapted to live in incredibly acidic water such as that found in the Rift Lakes of Africa. In this chapter you will learn the basics about how the habitats of fish are divided and what adaptations certain species have developed to survive in their unique environment.

The simplest division of habitats for fish is freshwater versus saltwater. This division does not take into account, however, the fact that many aquatic environments are neither fresh nor marine – they may be a combination of both (this is called brackish). In this chapter you will find a description of the various types of freshwater and marine habitats in which fish are found. You will also find detailed information regarding the geographical location of some of these habitats as well as lists of common fish species found in each habitat.

1) Freshwater Habitats

The term "freshwater" refers to a body of water having a salt concentration below 1 per cent. Organisms that have adapted to thrive in freshwater regions are generally incapable of surviving in the ocean or in other areas of high salt concentration. The three most prevalent freshwater regions are ponds and lakes, streams and rivers and wetlands.

a) Ponds and Lakes

The ponds and lakes of the world vary greatly in size from just a few square feet to spanning miles in diameter. Lakes are typically permanent bodies of water while ponds may come and go with the seasons. Because they are largely isolated from one another, ponds and lakes often have limited species diversity within but, also due to this isolation, some very unique adaptations are possible.

For example, Lake Tanganyika, the oldest lake in Africa (and possibly the world) is home to a wide variety of cichlid species. What is most interesting about these fish is that more than a dozen unique modern species evolved from a single species over the past 700,000 years. Furthermore, the fish living in such isolated environments tend to develop specialised adaptations to ensure access to food. Some fish develop keen eye sight to see through murky waters while others develop the ability to survive and thrive in the depths of the lake.

Like many bodies of water, pond and lakes are divided into "zones". The three zones of ponds and lakes are the littoral zone, the limnetic zone and the profundal zone. The littoral zone is the uppermost zone surrounding the edges of the pond or lake near the shoreline, this zone is typically the warmest and it is home to a variety of algae, snails, plants, fishes, crustaceans and amphibians. The water near the surface of the pond or lake surrounded by the littoral zone is called the limnetic zone.

The limnetic zone of any pond or lake is well exposed to sunlight which means that it is an ideal environment for the growth of algae and plankton. These plankton are essential food sources for other organisms in the pond or lake, particularly those that inhabit the profundal zone, the deeper waters. This area of the pond or lake is deeper and cooler because little light is able to penetrate the water's depth. Temperatures in all zones of a pond or lake are subject to seasonal variation.

4: Lake Tanganyika viewed from space

b) Streams and Rivers

A stream or river is a body of water that constantly flows in one direction. These bodies of water typically stem from a headwater and flow toward a larger body of water (such as another river or the ocean), fed by springs and snowmelt. Water temperatures in streams and rivers tend to be cooler toward the source where it is also clearer and richer in oxygen. The middle of any river or stream tends to exhibit the greatest species diversity. Toward the mouth of the river or stream, however, species diversity drops as the water becomes murky from displaced sediment and lower oxygen levels.

c) Wetlands

A wetland is an area of standing water such as a bog, marsh or swamp. These bodies of water tend to be rich in aquatic vegetation, particularly those like pond lilies and cattails that are adapted to very moist and humid conditions. Wetlands are not considered exclusively freshwater regions because saltwater marshes do exist. These marshes support different species than do freshwater marshes.

2) Saltwater Habitats

Saltwater" is a term used interchangeably with marine water and refers to the sea or ocean because they are environments with a high salt concentration. Saltwater covers about 75 per cent of the Earth's surface and the most prevalent saltwater regions include oceans, coral reefs and estuaries.

a) Oceans

An ocean is a very large body of saltwater and it is the largest of all Earthly ecosystems. Similar to lakes and ponds, oceans are also divided into zones: the intertidal, pelagic, abyssal and benthic zones. Though there are fewer species of animals living in oceans than on land, many researchers and scientists agree that oceans still support the greatest species diversity of any ecosystem on the planet.

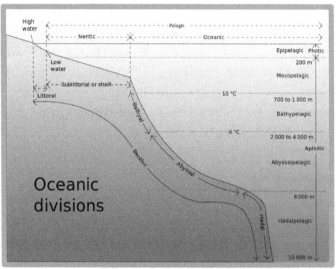

The intertidal zone is the outermost oceanic zone, located where the ocean meets the land. Because the tides move in and out throughout the course of the day, this zone is alternately submerged and exposed. Areas of the intertidal zone that are typically submerged are home to a variety of species of crabs, snails and small fish. A greater diversity of fishes and invertebrates can be found in the deeper portions of the intertidal zones, those areas which are only exposed at low tide.

The second oceanic zone is the pelagic zone which includes the surface level of the open ocean. Though close to the surface, this zone is typically cold. The pelagic zone is home to a variety of fish and mammals, including whales and dolphins which feed on the plankton that are abundant in this oceanic zone. Below the pelagic zone is the benthic zone which is also very cold and dark.

The benthic zone does not include the deepest waters of the ocean, but it does include layers of sand, silt and dead organisms. Here can be found a variety of organisms including fungi, bacteria, sea anemones, sea stars and fishes. Water temperatures continually decrease toward the deepest part of the ocean, the abyssal zone. The water in this zone is high in oxygen content and highly pressurized, but it is also very cold and low in nutrients. Despite the harshness of such an environment, the abyssal zone is still home to a variety of fish and invertebrates.

b) Coral Reefs

Coral reefs are underwater structures formed of thousands of tiny animals found in marine waters. Coral Reefs grow best in warm, shallow, sunny waters in the world's oceans, and are generally considered to represent some of the greatest species diversity in the world. Coral reefs are often found off the coast of continents, acting as barriers to the open ocean. Despite the diversity of life, coral reefs are actually fairly low in nutrients. Corals and other organisms living in these regions tend to obtain their nutrients through photosynthesis and through plankton in the water. Often fishes living near the Coral Reefs will adopt the colours of the Reef for camouflage, for example, the Clownfish.

c) Estuaries

An estuary is a body of water where a freshwater river or stream meets with an ocean, the result is a mixture of fresh and saltwater often referred to as "brackish". The salt concentration in these regions may vary so the organisms living in estuaries must be capable of adapting to a variable environment. The most common flora found in these areas include marsh grasses and mangrove trees while fauna can be very diverse, including many species of waterfowl, crabs, worms and fish.

3) Fish Habitats by Region

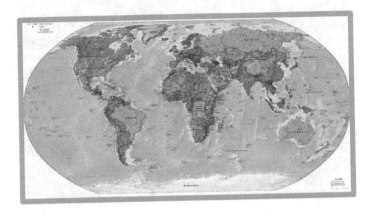

Earlier in this chapter you received some basic information about the different types of habitat in which fish can be found all over the world. In this section, however, you will receive more detailed information regarding where those habitats can be found as well as examples of the type of fish that live in these areas. This section of the book is split into six geographical regions, focusing on the most significant fish of those regions, including Asia, Africa, Australia, Caribbean, the Americas and Europe and the UK.

Fish of Asia

Asia is the largest continent on Earth and also the most heavily populated. This continent covers an area of nearly 45 million square kilometers (over 17 million square miles) and has a population of over 4 billion people. As the largest continent on Earth, the climate of Asia varies greatly by geographical location. Much of the interior of the continent is very dry while the southeast sections are very wet, heavily influenced by monsoons. The western sections of Asia are known for having some of the greatest daily temperature ranges.

The southern regions of Asia are typically warm to hot while the far northern regions, such as Siberia, are very cold. The eastern sections of the continent are fairly temperate. The southern portions of Asia, including the Indian subcontinent, are highly affected by monsoons, which account for approximately 80 per cent of the annual rainfall in some Asian countries, including India.

Asia is home to a number of freshwater bodies such as the Yangtze River in China and a variety of lakes. These bodies of water are home to the native freshwater fishes of Asia, many of which are popular in the aquarium trade. Some common freshwater fishes native to Asia include barbs, minnows, rasboras, tetras, perch, eel, gouramis and catfish. The largest saltwater bodies found in and around Asia are home to a number of marine species of fish including batfish, butterflyfish, bannerfish, surgeonfish, angelfish, jacks, barracuda, groupers and more.

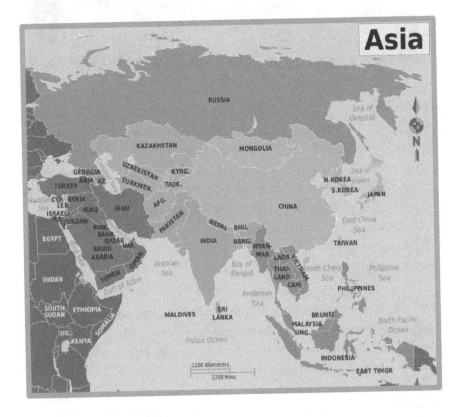

Parrotfish

Cetoscarus bicolour

Parrotfish

Subspecies Scientific Name:	*Cetoscarus bicolour*
Subspecies Domestic Name:	Bicolour Parrotfish
Habitat/Region:	Indian Ocean, Pacific Ocean, Red Sea
Size:	35 inches (90cm)
Conservation:	Safe

The bicolour parrotfish is one of the largest species of parrotfish, growing up to 35 inches (90cm) in length. These fish are unique in that they are sequential hermaphrodites, this means that they begin life s female and change into males later in life. During the early stages of life, the bicolour parrotfish has a dark brown body with a large cream-coloured patch on the upper part of the body. When the fish become male, they become very colourful overall, having green and pink spotting all over the body. Juveniles of the species typically have white bodies with a black spot on the dorsal fin and an orange stripe through the eye.

Squirrelfish
Sargocenron spiniferum

Squirrelfish
Subspecies Scientific Name: *Sargocentron spiniferum*
Subspecies Domestic Name: Sabre Squirrelfish
Habitat/Region: Indian Ocean, Pacific Ocean
Size: 18 to 20 inches (45 to 50cm)
Conservation: Safe

Also known as the giant squirrelfish or the spiny squirrelfish, this species is the largest species of squirrelfish. The sabre squirrelfish reaches a mature length between 18 and 20 inches (45 to 50 cm) and it is known for its bright red colour. These fish have very large eyes (because they are a nocturnal species) as well as a pointed snout and a protruding lower jaw. Sabre squirrelfish are native to the Indo-Pacific region and can be found all the way from the Red Sea and the Indian Ocean to Japan and Australia. This species tends to prefer shallow reef waters up to a depth of about 120 meters (400ft).

Cardinalfish

Pterapogon kauderni

Cardinalfish

Subspecies Scientific Name: *Pterapogon kauderni*
Subspecies Domestic Name: Banggai Cardinalfish
Habitat/Region: Indonesia; shallow waters
Size: 3 inches (8cm)
Conservation: Endangered

The Banggai cardinalfish is a small species of cardinalfish native to the Banggai islands of Indonesia. Because their natural range is so limited, these fish are considered to be endangered. This species tends to inhabit the shallow waters surrounding the islands of the Banggai Archipelago and their estimated population size is only about 2.4 million in total.

Banggai cardinalfish grow up to 3 inches (8cm) in length and have a deeply forked tail. This species exhibits three black bars along the head and body as well as white spots on the tail and fins. The Banggai cardinalfish is the only member of its family that is active during the day and it tends to travel in groups of 8 to 9 individuals.

Carp
Cyprinus carpio

Carp
Subspecies Scientific Name: *Cyprinus carpio*
Subspecies Domestic Name: Common Carp
Habitat/Region: Europe and Asia; rivers and lakes
Size: up to 50 lbs. (23kg)
Conservation: Safe

The common carp is native to the lakes and rivers in Europe and Asia, but it has been introduced in many other areas where it has come to be considered an invasive species. These fish belong to the family Cyprinidae and can grow to weigh 50 lbs. (23kg) or more, reaching a length up to 47 inches (120cm). In addition to growing very large, these fish can also live for 60 years or more. The common carp has a long, silver bodies with dark tints of colour with dark fins and red flesh.

Barb

Barbonymus schwanenfeldii

Barb

Subspecies Scientific Name:	*Barbonymus schwanenfeldii*
Subspecies Domestic Name:	Tinfoil Barb
Habitat/Region:	Asia
Size:	14 inches (35cm)
Conservation:	Safe

This species of fish is a member of the family Cyprinidae with other barbs as well as rasboras, danios, carp and minnows. The tinfoil barb is easily identifiable by its silver colouration with a red dorsal fin and orange or red caudal fin. These fish can grow up to 14 inches (35 cm) long and may live as long as 10 years. This species is popular in the aquarium trade as well as the fishing industry.

Fish of Africa

Africa is the second largest continent on the planet as well as the second most-populated. This continent covers a land area of about 30.2 million square kilometers (11.7 million square miles) which is equivalent to about 6 per cent of the Earth's total surface. Africa is bordered by the Mediterranean Sea to the north, the Red Sea to the northeast, the Atlantic Ocean to the west and the Indian Ocean to the southeast. Several large bodies of freshwater are also located on the continent such as the great Rift Valley lakes and the Nile River.

The climate of Africa ranges according to geographical location from tropical to subarctic. The northern half of the continent is primarily arid, or desert, while the southern half contains both savannah and rainforest regions. The highest recorded temperatures on Earth come from Africa. In 1922, Libya, was recorded with a temperature of 136°F (58°C).

The fauna of Africa is incredibly diverse with a very large number of endemic species, particularly in the Rift Valley lakes such as Lake Victoria and Lake Tanganyika. These lakes, as well as other freshwater bodies, are home to a variety of species of fish, including: cichlids, catfish, eel, lampeyes, tetras, pike and lungfish. The saltwater bodies surrounding Africa are home to marine species including hagfish, stingrays, herring, lancetfish, eels, toadfish, hake, anglers, pearlfish, lanternfish and more.

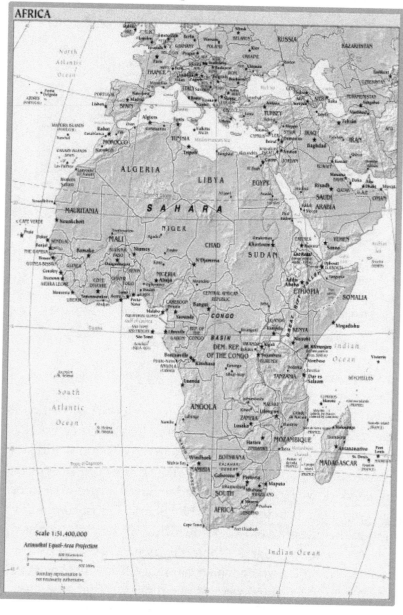

Great White Shark
Carcharodon carcharias

Great White Shark

Subspecies Scientific Name:	*Carcharodon carcharias*
Subspecies Domestic Name:	Great White Shark
Habitat/Region:	North America, Asia, Caribbean, Africa
Size:	13-17ft (4-5.3m), 1,500-2,430 lbs. (680-1,100kg)
Conservation:	Vulnerable

The Great White Shark is one of the largest species of shark with some measuring over 26 feet (8m) in length. These fierce predators can be found in the coastal areas of all the world's oceans in depths up to 3,900 feet (1,200m). They are most densely populated, however, off Dyer Island in South Africa. Classified as an epipelagic fish, the Great White Shark is most commonly found in the presence of rich game including sea lions, fur seals, large fish and other sharks – their only natural predator is the orca whale or killer whale which can range from 20-26 feet (5-8 metres) long and weigh in excess of 6 tonnes. What give sharks their name is their vast size as well as their colouration. Most specimens have a white underside with a grey-blue dorsal area.

Perhaps the most intimidating characteristic these fish have is their rows of large, serrated teeth designs to tear and shred flesh.

Stingray
Dasyatis pastinaca

Stingray
Subspecies Scientific Name: *Dasyatis pastinaca*
Subspecies Domestic Name: Common Stingray
Habitat/Region: Atlantic Ocean, Mediterranean Sea
Size: 18 inches (45cm)
Conservation: Safe

The common stingray is typically found in sandy or muddy waters in the Atlantic Ocean as well as in the Mediterranean and Black Seas. These fish often bury themselves in sediment where they find their main sources of food, mollusks, worms and small fishes. This species tends to reach an adult length around 18 inches (45cm) with a very long, whip-like tail. This tail contains a sharp, venomous spine which can cause serious pain, though the wound is typically not life-threatening. The population of this species is thought to be dwindling due to overfishing, though sufficient data is not available for the IUCN to perform a true assessment.

Killifish

Fundulopanchax gardneri

Killifish

Subspecies Scientific Name:	*Fundulopanchax gardneri*
Subspecies Domestic Name:	Blue Lyretail Killifish
Habitat/Region:	Africa; streams and marshes
Size:	2.25 inches (6cm)
Conservation:	Near Threatened

Native to the regions of Cameroon and Nigeria in Africa, the blue lyretail killifish inhabits streams and ponds. What makes killifish unique is that many species can survive long periods of time out of water – their eggs can also be dried. The blue lyretail killifish is named for its bright blue colouration and the pointed lyre-like shape of its tail.

Tilapia

Oreochromis niloticus

Tilapia

Subspecies Scientific Name:	*Oreochromis niloticus*
Subspecies Domestic Name:	Nile Tilapia
Habitat/Region:	Africa; streams, ponds, rivers, lakes
Size:	24 inches (60cm), 9.5lbs (4.3kg)
Conservation:	Safe

The common name Tilapia is given to almost one hundred different species of cichlids belonging to the order Perciformes. The Nile Tilapia is a native species in Africa, found from Egypt to Central Africa, primarily in shallow streams, rivers and lakes. This species has distinctive vertical striping on the body that extends to the tail. In addition to being popular for fishing, this species also feeds on mosquito larvae which may help with the fight against malaria in Africa.

Fish of Australia

Australia is a fairly large continent, covering over 7.5 million square kilometers (nearly 3 million square miles). Because it is so large, the climate of Australia varies greatly. Most of the continent has a semi-arid or desert climate, though the south-east and south-west portions have temperate climates and fertile soil. The northern portion of the continent enjoys a tropical climate. The climate of Australia is largely impacted by its low elevation, the shape of the continent itself, cold ocean currents coming in off the west coast and the dominance of high-pressure systems.

It is estimated that about 68 per cent of the fish found in Australia live in tropical marine environments and most of these species are found in inshore environments (such as the reef). Less than 6 per cent of fishes native to Australia are found in fresh water and many of those species can also survive in estuarine or marine environments. In total, nearly 25 per cent of Australian fish species are endemic which means that they cannot naturally be found anywhere else on the planet. Freshwater endemism is the most prevalent followed marine and then estuarine environments.

The Murray-Darling Basin is the most important freshwater system in Australia. This particular body of water contains many of the continent's freshwater species including its largest freshwater fish, the Murray Cod. Other freshwater fish found in Australia, include: bass, grayling, smelt, catfish, perch, galaxias, rainbowfish, eel and gudgeon. As mentioned above, the majority of Australian fish species are found in marine environments. Some common types of marine fish in Australia include angelfish, butterflyfish, cardinalfish, clownfish, parrotfish, damselfish, goby, wrasse, groupers, trout and more.

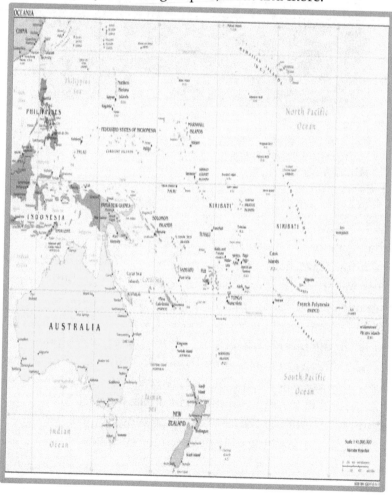

Tang
Paracanthurus hepatus

Tang
Subspecies Scientific Name:	*Paracanthurus hepatus*
Subspecies Domestic Name:	Regal Tang
Habitat/Region:	Indian Ocean, Pacific Ocean, Reefs
Size:	12 inches (30cm)
Conservation:	Safe

Perhaps one of the most iconic species of tang, the regal tang is known for its brilliant blue colouration with black patterning and yellow tail. These fish are also known by the names blue tang and palette surgeonfish. Regal tangs are naturally found throughout the Indo-Pacific region and they are incredibly popular in the marine aquarium hobby. The regal tang has a very flat body with a circular shape. These fish grow up to 12 inches (30cm) long and they have very small scales. Though these fish can be found in a variety of different areas, they are not "common" in any particular area. According to the IUCN, the regal tang is not a vulnerable or endangered species.

Butterflyfish
Chaetodon ephippium

Butterflyfish

Subspecies Scientific Name:	*Chaetodon ephippium*
Subspecies Domestic Name:	Saddle Butterflyfish
Habitat/Region:	Indian Ocean, Pacific Ocean, Australia
Size:	12 inches (30cm)
Conservation:	Safe

This species of butterfly fish is found throughout the Indo-Pacific region ranging all the way from Sri Lanka to Hawaii and south to Australia. These fish are very large, growing up to 12 inches (30cm) in length. Similar in shape the angelfish, the saddle butterflyfish has an overall colour of yellowish gray with a large black spot bordered with a white band. These fish also have wavy blue lines running horizontally along the lower half of the body. This species can be found in coral reefs up to 30 meters deep, feeding on various types of algae and invertebrates.

Clownfish

Amphiprion ocellaris

Clownfish

Subspecies Scientific Name:	*Amphiprion ocellaris*
Subspecies Domestic Name:	Ocellaris Clownfish
Habitat/Region:	Australia; Great Barrier Reef
Size:	4.3 inches (11cm)
Conservation:	Safe

Also known as the common clownfish or the false percula clownfish, this species is one of the most popular species of marine aquarium fish. The ocellaris clownfish can be found in many marine habitats all over the world and its colouration varies depending on geographical location. In Australia and Southeast Asia, for example, these fish are black with white bands. In other areas, however, this species may be orange or reddish-brown in colour with three wide white bands. Though females typically grow larger than males, the maximum size for this fish is only about 4.3 inches (11cm). These fish have a stocky body shape with a rounded profile. They can be found living in anemones in reefs and sheltered lagoons, often in small groups, at a maximum water depth of 15 meters (49 ft.).

Angelfish

Pygoplites diacanthus

Angelfish

Subspecies Scientific Name:	*Pygoplites diacanthus*
Subspecies Domestic Name:	Royal Angelfish
Habitat/Region:	Indian Ocean, Pacific Ocean
Size:	10 inches (25cm)
Conservation:	Safe

Known as both the royal angelfish and the regal angelfish, this species can be found throughout the Indo-Pacific region in tropical areas. The royal angelfish is often sold in the aquarium hobby, but it is very difficult to keep alive in captivity because they often refuse to eat anything they are offered. In the wild, these fish are known to grow up to 10 inches (25cm) long and they are easily distinguished by their bright colouration. With alternating bands of black, white and orange, these fish are easy to spot – their fins are bright blue with a bold yellow tail.

Wrasse

Pseudocheilinus hexataenia

Wrasse

Subspecies Scientific Name:	*Pseudocheilinus hexataenia*
Subspecies Domestic Name:	Six-Line Wrasse
Habitat/Region:	Indian Ocean, Pacific Ocean
Size:	4 inches (10cm)
Conservation:	Safe

The six-line wrasse is native to the Indian and Pacific Oceans where it can be found in reefs and other coastal areas. These fish grow to about 4 inches (10cm) in length and they tend to inhabit areas ranging from 3 to 115 feet (1 to 35m) deep. This species of wrasse is named for its lined pattern which runs horizontally along the body. The main body colour is orange, ornamented with six distinct blue lines. During courting, males of the species develop increased intensity in their colour to attract a mate.

Bream

Abramis brama

Bream

Subspecies Scientific Name:	*Abramis brama*
Subspecies Domestic Name:	Common Bream
Habitat/Region:	Australia
Size:	22 inches (55cm), 8.8lbs (4kg)
Conservation:	Safe

The common bream is a European species of fish belonging to the family Cyprinidae. These fish typically inhabit ponds, lakes and canals, though they can also be found in slow-moving rivers. The common bream grows to an average length of 12 to 22 inches (30 to 55cm) long and can weigh between 4.4 and 8.8 lbs. (2 to 4 kg). This species has a flat body with silver-gray colouration on the body and fins.

Cod

Maccullochella peelii

Cod

Subspecies Scientific Name:	*Maccullochella peelii*
Subspecies Domestic Name:	Murray Cod
Habitat/Region:	Australia; rivers
Size:	32 to 39 inches (80 to 100cm)
Conservation:	Critically Endangered

The Murray Cod is a grouper-like fish, also known by the names greenfish and goodoo. These fish are not only the largest freshwater fish in Australia but also one of the largest in the world. Though the average specimen grows to about 39 inches (100cm), these fish are capable of growing to more than 3 feet (1m) in length and can weigh over 200 lbs. (91kg). Unfortunately, populations have declined severely due to overfishing and habitat degradation.

Fish of the Caribbean

The Caribbean is a region located southeast of the Gulf of Mexico, east of Central America and north of South America. Made up of more than 700 islands, reefs and cays, this region has a total land area around 92,500 square miles (240,000 square kilometers). The overall climate of this region is tropical but rainfall varies by geographical location. Sunshine is consistent throughout the year, though the last six months of the year tend to get more rain than the first six.

Though some islands have their own freshwater sources, most of the fish species found in the Caribbean can be found in the Caribbean Sea or in the Atlantic Ocean. The Puerto Rico trench, the deepest point in the Atlantic Ocean, is found in the Caribbean region and the Caribbean Sea is home to a wide variety of fish species. Some types of marine fish found in the Caribbean include angelfish, butterflyfish, surgeonfish, barracuda, grunt, chub, chromis, snapper, damselfish and more. Freshwater species are much fewer in number, including snook, river goby, minnows, killifish, anchovy, gambusia and mullet.

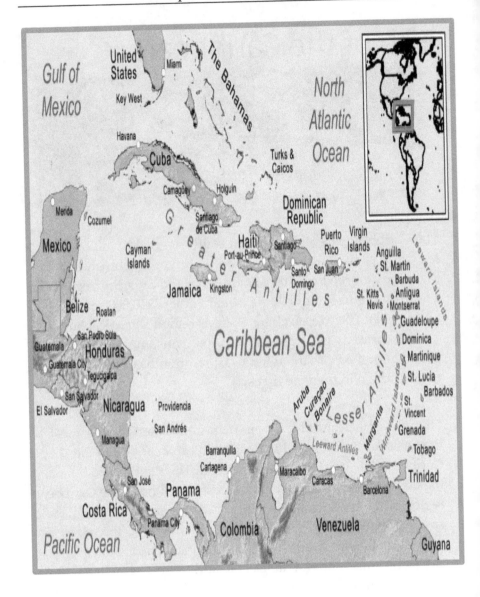

Lionfish

Pterois volitans

Lionfish

Subspecies Scientific Name:	*Pterois volitans*
Subspecies Domestic Name:	Red Lionfish
Habitat/Region:	Indian Ocean, Pacific Ocean, Caribbean Sea
Size:	18.5 inches (47cm)
Conservation:	Safe

The red lionfish is native to the Indo-Pacific region but it has become an invasive species throughout the Caribbean Sea as well as along the eastern coast of the United States. These fish are coloured with red and white stripes, having long spiny fins. The red lionfish typically grows to about 18.5 inches (47cm) long and they can live as long as 10 years. These fish received their name from the fact that their spines are arranged in a mane-like fashion around the head. These spines are venomous but are typically used for Defence, not to attack prey.

Damselfish

Stegastes variabilis

Damselfish

Subspecies Scientific Name:	*Stegastes variabilis*
Subspecies Domestic Name:	Coco Damselfish
Habitat/Region:	Caribbean Sea, Atlantic Ocean; reefs
Size:	5 inches (12.5cm)
Conservation:	Safe

The cocoa damselfish can be found in coral reefs and rocky reefs throughout the Caribbean Sea and in parts of the Atlantic Ocean, including the Gulf of Mexico. These fish have oval-shaped, laterally compressed bodies and grow to a maximum length of about 5 inches (12.5cm) long. Adults of this species are divided in colour – bright blue or brown on the top half and yellow on the bottom half. The sides of the fish are marked with fine dark bars with two small black spots above the pectoral fins. During breeding season, females of the species they their eggs where they can attach to shells and empty stones. Males of the species then fertilise and guard the eggs until they hatch.

Goatfish
Mulloidichthys vanicolensis

Goatfish

Subspecies Scientific Name:	*Mulloidichthys vanicolensis*
Subspecies Domestic Name:	Yellowfin Goatfish
Habitat/Region:	Indian Ocean, Pacific Ocean
Size:	15 inches (38cm)
Conservation:	Safe

This species of goatfish is native to the Indian and Pacific Oceans ranging all the way from the Red Sea to Hawaii, even as far north as Japan. The yellowfin goatfish is typically found in reef areas, though it can also be found in lagoons and waters between 1 and 113 meters (3 to 370ft) deep. This species swims in large groups by day and, at night, hunts for worms and crustaceans. As suggested by the name, the yellowfin goatfish has yellow fins and a yellow longitudinal band running along the body. The rest of the body is white in colour with a blue-green sheen.

Fish of Europe and UK

Europe is the sixth largest continent on the planet and contains 47 different countries. This continent is bordered by several bodies of water and it is separated from its neighboring continent, Asia, by the Ural Mountains and by the Black and Caspian Seas. Europe has a temperate, continental climate for the most part, though some areas on the western coast have a maritime climate and the countries in the south have a Mediterranean climate. The Gulf Stream keeps the air mild in high-latitude regions such as the UK, Ireland and Norway.

Because numerous bodies of water can be found in and around Europe, the freshwater and marine wildlife is greatly varied. Some of the most popular freshwater species for fishing and human consumption include brown trout, rainbow trout, carp, pike, stickleback, bream, perch and barbell. Common marine species native to European waters include anchovy, cod, hake, herring, sole, mackerel, turbot, plaice, Atlantic salmon and Bluefin tuna.

Flounder
Bothus mancus

Flounder

Subspecies Scientific Name:	*Bothus mancus*
Subspecies Domestic Name:	Peacock Flounder
Habitat/Region:	Indian Ocean, Pacific Ocean
Size:	18 inches (45cm)
Conservation:	Safe

The peacock flounder, also known as the flowery flounder, is found in shallow waters throughout the Indo-Pacific region. These fish have flat bodies with both eyes located on the top left side of the head. In juveniles, the eyes are located on either side of the head but one eventually moves to the left side, enabling the fish to lie flat on the bottom of the ocean and to look both backward and forward at the same time. These fish received their nickname flowery flounder for the blue flower-like spots covering the body. The peacock flounder reaches a maximum length at maturity around 18 inches (45cm).

Perch

Perca fluviatilis

Perch

Subspecies Scientific Name: *Perca fluviatilis*
Subspecies Domestic Name: European Perch
Habitat/Region: Europe and Asia; lakes and ponds
Size: under 24 inches (60cm)
Conservation: Safe

This species of fish is predatory, feeding on insects as well as small fish. The European perch is very popular among anglers and, as such, has been introduced to many other areas including Australia and South Africa. Unfortunately, because these fish are predators they can do great damage to native fish populations. The size of this species varies, but the largest recorded was 24 inches (60cm) long.

Trout

Salmo trutta

Trout

Subspecies Scientific Name:	*Salmo trutta*
Subspecies Domestic Name:	Brown Trout
Habitat/Region:	Europe (Wles); rivers and lakes
Size:	up to 20 lbs. (9kg)
Conservation:	Safe

The brown trout is a non-migratory species that is very popular for fishing. These fish have brown colouration with dark spots on the body. The largest specimen of this species weighed in at 31 lbs. 12 oz., caught in March 2005. Though they can get very large, brown trout do not grow quickly. Interestingly, the brown trout is capable of interbreeding with sea trout – this is uncommon, however, due to the fact that the two live in very different habitats.

Fish of the Americas

North and South America stretch from the icy Artic to the stormy coast of Cape Horn, then into the Southern Ocean. The Caribbean Sea borders the southeast portion of the continent.

North America

The total land area of North America is nearly 10 million square miles (almost 25 million square kilometers).

Because it is such a large land mass, the climate of North America differs from one geographical location to another. In the northernmost regions of Canada and Alaska, subarctic and tundra climates prevail while, in the southern United States the climate is tropical and subtropical. The majority of the interior of the continent enjoys temperate climates, ranging toward semiarid and arid conditions in the west.

The North American continent is bordered by several large bodies of saltwater, so it is home to a wide variety of marine fish species and freshwater fish. For example, the world's smallest shark, the dogfish can be found in the marine waters of North America.

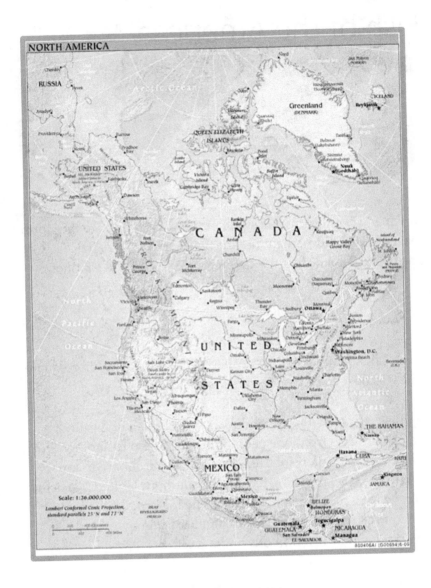

Dogfish

Squalus acanthias

Dogfish

Subspecies Scientific Name:	*Squalus acanthias*
Subspecies Domestic Name:	Spiny Dogfish
Habitat/Region:	Europe, North America, Australia
Size:	2.5 to 3.3 ft. (80 to 100cm)
Conservation:	Threatened

The spiny dogfish is known by several names including the mud shark or piked dogfish. This species is one of the most well-known species of dogfish and they are found throughout the world in shallow offshore waters. The spiny dogfish can be distinguished from other species because it has two spines, one behind each dorsal fin, but no anal fin. These fish also have white spots running along the back. The spiny dogfish is used for food throughout Europe as well as in North America and Australia. In addition to the meat, the fins of these fish are sold to make shark fin soup, a type of Chinese cuisine.

Snapper

Lutjanus campechanus

Snapper

Subspecies Scientific Name:	*Lutjanus campechanus*
Subspecies Domestic Name:	Red Snapper
Habitat/Region:	North America; Atlantic Ocean
Size:	39 inches (100cm), 50 lbs. (22.8kg)
Conservation:	Safe

This species is native to the western Atlantic Ocean, including the Gulf of Mexico, and it can be found in reef areas. In addition to being popular as a game fish, the red snapper is also commercially significant. This species is named for its red colouration. These fish have laterally compressed bodies with a sloped profile. They can reach up to 39 inches (100cm) and may weigh up to 50 lbs. (22.8kg). Though these fish have sharp teeth, they do not have upper canine teeth like other types of snapper including the mutton snapper and the dog snapper. Another distinguishing feature of this species is the spiny rays on its dorsal and anal fins.

Goby

Rhinogobiops nicholsii

Goby

Subspecies Scientific Name: *Rhinogobiops nicholsii*
Subspecies Domestic Name: Blackeye Goby
Habitat/Region: North America; Pacific Ocean
Size: 6 inches (15cm)
Conservation: Safe

Also known as the bluespot goby or the crested goby, the blackeye goby is the only species belonging to the genus Rhinogobiops. This species is often white in colour, though it can range all the way to a dark purplish brown. The most distinctive feature of this species is the dark black spot on the dorsal fins and the iridescent blue spot beneath each eye. What makes these fish unique is their ability to rapidly change colour in response to threats. This is particularly common in mating situations, as this species is highly territorial. These fish remain fairly small, generally reaching about 6 inches (15cm) in adulthood. Compared to the size of their bodies, the blackeye goby has very large eyes.

Catfish
Ameiurus melas

Catfish

Subspecies Scientific Name:	*Ameiurus melas*
Subspecies Domestic Name:	Black Bullhead
Habitat/Region:	North America; slow-moving waters
Size:	6-10 inches (15-25cm)
Conservation:	Safe

Found throughout the central United States, the black bullhead tends to inhabit stagnant and slow-moving waters. These fish congregate around dams and lake outlets, liking habitats with soft bottoms and muddy water. Black bullheads will eat almost anything they can find and they reproduce quickly, laying as many as 6,000 eggs at once. This species has a flat head, squared tail and humped back.

South America

South America is a continent bordered on the north and east by the Atlantic Ocean and by the Pacific Ocean on the west. This continent covers an area of nearly 18 million square kilometers (nearly 7 million square miles). This continent is predominantly hot and moist, though the climate varies slightly by geographical region. It is home to such fish as the notorious piranha, which can be found in its freshwaters and the beautiful butterfly fish in its marine waters and more.

Hatchetfish

Carnegiella marthae

Hatchetfish

Subspecies Scientific Name:	*Carnegiella marthae*
Subspecies Domestic Name:	Black-Winged Hatchetfish
Habitat/Region:	South America; streams and pools
Size:	1.5 inches (4cm)
Conservation:	Safe

Hatchetfish belong to the order Characiformes and there are nine different freshwater species. The black-winged hatchetfish is named for its black colour and the wing-like shape of its pectoral fins. These fish typically inhabit the calm streams and pools of the Orinoco and Negro Rivers in South America. What makes hatchetfish unique is their ability to jump out of the water to catch insects.

Guppy
Poecilia reticulata

Guppy

Subspecies Scientific Name:	*Poecilia reticulata*
Subspecies Domestic Name:	Fancy Guppy
Habitat/Region:	South America; streams, rivers and ponds
Size:	1.5 inches (3.5cm)
Conservation:	Safe

Also known as the rainbow fish and the million fish, the guppy is one of the most popular species of freshwater fish in the aquarium hobby. These little fish only grow to about 1.5 inches (3.5cm) long but they exhibit brilliant colours and long, flowing fins. Guppies come in all colours and patterns, produced in countless strains through selective breeding.

Piranha
Pygocentrus natterei

Piranha

Subspecies Scientific Name:	*Pygocentrus natterei*
Subspecies Domestic Name:	Red-Bellied Piranha
Habitat/Region:	South America; rivers and basins
Size:	13 inches (33cm), 7.7 lbs. (3.5kg)
Conservation:	Safe

Though commonly regarded as ferocious predators, the piranha is actually an omnivore, feeding on insects and crustaceans as well as other fish. These fish tend to live in shoals (groups) but rarely hunt as a group. This species have thick bodies with dark colouration and a red tinge on the belly. The maximum size for these fish is 13 inches (33cm) with a maximum weight of 7.7 lbs. (3.5kg).

Rasbora

Trigonostigma heteromorpha

Rasbora

Subspecies Scientific Name:	*Trigonostigma heteromorpha*
Subspecies Domestic Name:	Harlequin Rasbora
Habitat/Region:	South America; rivers and basins
Size:	2 inches (5cm)
Conservation:	Safe

The harlequin rasbora was named for the unique shape of its body as well as the triangular black marking on the body near the tail. These fish are very popular in the aquarium hobby and it is often confused with other related species that look very similar. The harlequin rasbora inhabits the streams and swampy waters of Asia though they can easily be kept in community tanks with many South American species due to the similarity of their habitat requirements.

Tetra

Paracheirodon axelrodi

Tetra

Subspecies Scientific Name:	*Paracheirodon axelrodi*
Subspecies Domestic Name:	Cardinal Tetra
Habitat/Region:	South America; rivers
Size:	1.25 inches (3cm)
Conservation:	Safe

Named for its bright red colouration, the cardinal tetra is one of the most popular species of freshwater aquarium fish. These fish are related to the neon tetra, also popular, and exhibit a similar bright blue line running horizontally along the body. This species was once difficult to breed in captivity but, since that is no longer the case, it is becoming increasingly easy to find.

Acara

Andinoacara pulcher

Acara

Subspecies Scientific Name:	*Andinoacara pulcher*
Subspecies Domestic Name:	Blue Acara
Habitat/Region:	South America
Size:	6 inches (15cm)
Conservation:	Safe

Named for their brilliant blue colouration, the Blue Acara is a member of the cichlid family. This species can be found throughout Central and South America, typically in streams and other small bodies of water. The Blue Acara typically reaches around 6 inches (15 cm) and they have stocky, compact bodies with long, flowing fins. Perhaps the most attractive feature of these fish is the dark vertical bars on their bodies as well as horizontal lines of blue-green scales which give the fish the appearance of sparkling.

Pacu

Colossoma macropomum

Pacu

Subspecies Scientific Name:	*Colossoma macropomum*
Subspecies Domestic Name:	Black Pacu
Habitat/Region:	South America
Size:	36 inches (1m), 88 lbs. (40kg)
Conservation:	Safe

Also known as the tambaqui, the black pacu is the largest species of characin (member of the order Characiformes) in South America. These fish inhabit the Amazon and Orinoco River basins, though they have been introduced throughout the continent. Black pacu can grow over 3 ft. (1m) long and can weigh as much as 88 lbs. (40kg). These fish are dark in colouration, as suggested by their name, and they feed primarily on plants, zooplankton and insects.

Chapter Five: Conservation Concerns

Though fish are some of the most common animals on the planet, they are still in danger from habitat destruction, overfishing and other conservation concerns. Fish have existed on this planet for more than 500 million years, so it is a shame to think that even one of the many modern species might die out at the hands of humans. In this chapter you will learn the basics about conservation concerns in regard to fish. You will also learn some practical ways in which you can help to mitigate your own impact on the threat to fish and some steps you can take to suppose conservation efforts in your area.

1) Habitat Destruction

Perhaps the most devastating conservation concern for fish all over the world is habitat destruction. Habitat destruction affects fish in both freshwater and marine environments, largely due to man-made stresses. As human populations and industries expand, natural habitats like estuaries, swamps and wetlands are being destroyed to make room. The animals living in these habitats may be killed outright or they could die slowly due to a lack of food and shelter that was once abundantly available.

a) Threats to Freshwater Ecosystems

Not only is fresh water essential to human survival, but it is estimated that freshwater sources are home to more than 40 per cent of the world's fish species. According to National Geographic, more than 20 per cent of the world's known freshwater fish species have become threatened or extinct in the past few decades alone. This is largely due to human influence in the form of pollution, habitat disruption and invasion of exotic species.

Some of the most pressing conservation concerns affecting freshwater environments include:

- Runoff from urban and agricultural areas.
- Draining wetlands for development.
- Withdrawal of water for human use.
- Disruption of habitats through water-diversion systems. (eg, dams)
- Pollution of groundwater supplies.
- Introduction and invasion of exotic species.

Agricultural Expansion

As human populations increase, their need for space increases as well. Industrial development and agricultural expansion results in a need for deforestation and other means of habitat destruction. While deforestation may not directly affect fish, increased runoff due to the destruction of forests does – deforestation can lead to increased runoff which may increase the sediment load in rivers and lakes. Sedimentation can decrease visibility in the water, making it more difficult for fish to locate food – it can also result in loss of habitat.

Water Pollution

One of the most significant consequences of human expansion is pollution. Runoff from agricultural and industrial areas, dumping of waste and pollution of groundwater can have a serious impact on the quality of natural water supplies. One of the most significant conservation problems affecting the planet's water sources today is eutrophication. Eutrophication is the term used to describe an ecosystem's response to the addition of either natural or artificial substances (ex: sewage and fertiliser).

The term 'hypertophication' can also be used in place of eutrophication because it depicts one of the most common environmental responses to water pollution: an increase in plant biomass. As natural water sources become affected by different forms of pollution (both natural and artificial), it leads to an increase in the nutrients plants need to grow (namely nitrogen and phosphorus). As a result, the plant biomass of the ecosystem dramatically increases which can lead to changes in water chemistry, availability of nutrients and loss of species diversity.

Another example of water pollution is the use of agricultural pesticides. These chemicals are used to protect crops from damaging insects but the runoff from these chemicals can be toxic to local fauna. Mining activity can also produce harmful pollutants such as lead, iron and copper which often leak into sewage systems and then into ground water supplies as well as rivers and lakes. These chemicals will only cause more of a problem in the future through the process of bioaccumulation.

Water Extraction

You may have heard the statistic that water covers nearly 75 per cent of the planet, but that water is not evenly distributed. In Africa, for example, 50 per cent of the total surface water on the entire continent is found in the Congo River basin alone. In areas such as this, water must be transported to populated areas for human use and consumption. The transfer of water has numerous detrimental impacts on the local environment such as reduced flow in donor rivers, increased flow in recipient rivers, chemical changes in water quality, spread of invasive species, exposure to disease and physical changes to the environment.

b) Threats to Marine Environments

As is true for freshwater environments, the most pressing conservation concern for marine environments is habitat loss. In addition to this issue, however, are concerns with damaging fishing methods, climate change and pollution.

Habitat Destruction

While humans get most of the blame for habitat destruction, there are also some natural factors to consider. Hurricanes, tsunamis, typhoons and other natural disasters can have a significant (though typically temporary) effect on oceanic habitats. Human-orchestrated disruptions of habitat are, however, more persistent and damaging. All of the world's freshwater eventually leads to the ocean, so all types of pollution and freshwater habitat loss eventually have an impact on marine habitat destruction as well.

Inland dams can disrupt fish migration routes and can cut off freshwater flow, thus increasing the salinity of coastal water. Deforestation, even in areas far from the shore, can create erosion that leads to sedimentation in shallow waters and reefs. Even tourism has an effect on habitat destruction as boaters and scuba divers come into direct contact with fragile oceanic ecosystems. Dumping of sewage and oil spills can cause damage that lasts for years.

Damaging Fishing Methods

While the key concern with fishing is overharvesting, fishing can also have an impact on the environment itself. In an article written by S.J. Turner, et al. published in the *Journal of Fisheries Management and Ecology,* Turner explains that certain fishing activities can cause degradation of the environment. For example, trawling and dredging practices used to harvest fish and shellfish often involve dragging fishing gear along the seabed. These practices result in the alteration of the physical aspects of the habitat and may also lead to changes in sediment suspension and chemistry. According to the article, these disturbances take much longer for the environment and its inhabitants to recover from than natural disturbances such as waves and storms.

Climate Change

The effects of climate change are vast and significant but the world's oceans may be the most affected. As the temperature of the Earth rises, it is its oceans that absorb the extra heat. As ice caps and glaciers melt, sea levels rise and estuaries become flooded. The ocean is a delicate environment, so even the slightest changes in water temperature or chemistry can have a significant and lasting impact on its inhabitants.

2) Overfishing

The term "overfishing" is generally used in reference to the taking of wildlife from a body of water at a rate that is too high to sustain. If the number of fish removed from a body of water exceeds the ability of the species to replenish itself, it can become a serious problem. One of the first problems with overfishing occurred during the 1800s when whales were overfished for the use of their blubber in lamp oil. Since then, numerous species including Atlantic cod and herring have been fished nearly to the brink of extinction. Not only does overfishing affect the existence of the species being fished, but it can also disrupt the food chain.

Overfishing, or overharvesting, is a problem in both freshwater and marine environments but it is most commonly mentioned in regard to the ocean. During the mid-20th century, an increase in interest of fish as a healthy protein source led to a sudden increase in fishing. Commercial fishing fleets began to use aggressive fishing methods to find and extract their target species to make them available for sale.

By 1989, however, over 90 million tons of fish had been extracted from the world's oceans and several species including the Chilean sea bass and Bluefin tuna have become more difficult to find. A study conducted in 2003 revealed that populations of large ocean fish have been reduced to a mere 10 per cent of their pre-industrial population due to the increase in industrial fishing practices. The problem is only projected to get worse as industrial fleets travel deeper into the ocean, moving further down the food chain to make their catches. A study conducted in 2006 by researchers at Dalhousie University in Nova Scotia and published in the journal *Science* predicts that by the year 2048, all of the world's fisheries will have collapsed due to overfishing.

As annual catch data returns smaller and smaller yields, we are beginning to understand that the world's oceans may be vast but they are not as unending as we once assumed. In conjunction with pollution, climate change and habitat destruction, overfishing has done irreparable damage to the world's stock of fish in both freshwater and marine environments. Some scientists argue that fish populations can be restored with aggressive changes to fishery management and the increased use of aquaculture, but it will not be a quick fix. Illegal fishing and unsustainable harvesting practices will always be an issue.

3) Other Conservation Concerns

Though habitat destruction and overfishing may be two of the most prevalent conservation concerns affecting fish, they are not the only problems. Some other concerns including invasive species and habitat disruption.

a) Invasive Species

The introduction of alien species into any environment can be incredibly damaging. For example, you may be familiar with the Pentatomidae family of insects – more commonly known as stink bugs. These insects have become agricultural pests, reproducing in large numbers and threatening all kinds of crops. Though stink bugs do not pose a threat to fish, other types of invasive species can and have had an effect on their environment and their survival.

Take Lake Victoria in Africa for example. Prior to the 1970s, this lake was home to more than 500 species of fish in the cichlid family alone and 90 per cent of those species were endemic (found only in Lake Victoria). Within the past few decades, however, the introduction of Nile Perch and Nile Tilapia for fishing purposes has greatly reduced the species diversity in the lake – nearly half the species that once existed are now extinct of threatened. While cichlids once comprised 80 per cent of the fish biomass of the lake, the Nile Perch alone currently comprises 60 per cent.

More recently, in late 2013, a major epidemic occurring in the Atlantic Ocean was brought to light. Lionfish (pictured above) are a species of venomous marine fish that have a tendency to eat and reproduce quickly and aggressively. These fish are not native to the Atlantic Ocean but they have been introduced into the environment, possibly by irresponsible pet owners. Having no natural predators aside from humans, lionfish can have an incredible impact on biodiversity, destroying up to 90 per cent of a reef. According to Graham Maddocks, the president and founder of the Ocean Support Foundation, "the lionfish invasion is probably the worst environmental disaster the Atlantic will ever face."

b) Habitat Disruption

According to the IUCN Red List, infrastructure development is the primary source of threat for crabs and the third largest threat to fish in Africa. Though the statistics of this study are limited to Africa, the reality is that habitat disruption occurs all over the world. Perhaps the most significant source of habitat disruption to affect fish is the building of dams and other forms of infrastructure development. In Africa alone there are more than 1,300 medium- to large-sized dams which directly affect about 4 per cent of Africa's freshwater animals.

Not only does the construction of a dam cause some level of damage to the environment, but it also creates some very drastic changes. Building a dam may stop or redirect the flow of a moving body of water which, as a result, creates a new wetland. Wetlands are an important type of aquatic environment, but not necessarily one to which the local flora and fauna are adapted. The building of a dam might prevent the migration or dispersal of fishes and other species which could ultimately lead to irreversible species loss in the area.

4) Conservation Societies and Zoos

Conservation of freshwater and marine life is a key concern all over the world and many organisations exist to help protect threatened species. For example, the Marine Conservation Society is the UK's leading charity dedicated to the protection and conservation of seas, shores and marine wildlife. Other notable conservation societies include:

GreenPeace International – dedicated to increasing awareness of and combating the top three threats to the world's oceans: overfishing, whaling and intensive shrimp aquaculture.

International Fund for Animal Welfare (IFAW) – partners with like-minded organisations to produce long-lasting solutions to conservation challenges

Oceana – an international non-profit organisation dedicated to protecting the planet's oceans through science, law, education and political advocacy

Reefbase – an organisation started to help facilitate the sustainable management of coral reefs and related marine environments

World Wildlife Fund (WWF) – an organisation that works to protect wildlife all over the world: the WWF Endangered Seas Program is present in more than 40 countries, helping to develop, campaign and advocate solutions for marine conservation

Marine Life Information Network (MarLIN) – an organisation in Britain and Ireland that works to provide information about marine environment management and protection

5) SEA LIFE London Aquarium and Volunteering

In addition to these organisations, zoos and aquariums all over the world help to promote education about conservation issues. As home to one of Europe's largest collections of marine life, SEA LIFE at the London Aquarium is an excellent example of this. In addition to providing education and support for global conservation issues, SEA LIFE also helps with local conservation through breeding programs, marine rescues and rehoming programs, as well as political and educational campaigns.

The London Aquarium is a wonderful place to go to view and enjoy the diversity of marine life found in the world's oceans, but that is not all it is good for. It is also a great place to go if you are looking for ways to get involved in conservation issues yourself. Volunteering at the London Aquarium is a great place to start. Visit their website for more information about volunteering opportunities as well as information about their current campaigns and the charities they partner with:

London Aquarium – Protect Our Seas
<http://www.visitsealife.com/london/protect-our-seas/>

A few campaigns the London Aquarium is currently active in include:

- **Make a Turtle Smile** – supports the construction of a sea turtle rescue center on Zakynthos

- **Seal Rescues** – the sister brand of SEA LIFE, Seal Sanctuaries, rescues and cares for over 100 orphaned seals each year before returning them to the wild

- **SEA HAPPY** – dedicated to raising funds for the protection of sea life as well as various breeding and rescue programs

- **Marine Stewardship Council (MSC)** – provides education regarding sustainable seafood

- **Shark Conservation** – provides information about dangerous practices like "shark finning"

- **Penguin Conservation** – dedicated to the preservation of Gentoo penguins in particular

Chapter Six: Species of Fish

There are an estimated 32,000 species of fish currently in existence. Having evolved over 500 million years ago, however, the number of fish that exist today is just a fraction of the number that have existed throughout the history of the world. In order to understand fish, you do not necessarily need to read a list of every species in existence. Rather, you should learn the basics about how fish are classified and categorized. Once you know the basics of fish classification, you can begin to understand the differences between the various groups and species.

1) Five Classes of Fish

Taxonomically, fish are divided into five classes but only three of those classes are currently in existence. The five classes of fish are as follows:

Agnatha – jawless fish

Osteichthyes – bony fish

Chondricthyes – cartilaginous fish

Placodermi – armored fish (extinct)

Acanthodii – spiny sharks (extinct)

Agnatha – this class of jawless fish can be further divided into two subclasses: Cyclostomata and Ostracodermi. The extinct species of fish belonging to this group are paraphyletic, meaning that all species diverged from a common ancestor. The oldest fossils of fish belonging to this class date back to the Cambrian period (which lasted from 541 to 485 million years ago). Two groups belonging to this class consisting of around 120 species still exist today: lampreys and hagfish.

Osteichthyes – this group of fishes is typically referred to as "bony fish" because they have bone rather than cartilage. This group consists of 45 different orders, more than 435 families and about 28,000 species, making it the largest taxonomical class in existence today. The Osteichthyes group can be further divided into two subclasses: Actinopterygii and Sarcopterygii.

The Actinopterygii class contains ray-finned fishes which are named for the fact that they have spiny "rays" supporting webs of skin for fins rather than the traditional fleshy fins of the Sarcopterygii class. Fish belonging to this subclass can be found in both freshwater and saltwater environments and currently existing species range in size from 0.3 inches (8mm) to 36 feet (11m) long. The Sarcopterygii subclass, as mentioned, is also referred to as lobe-finned fishes because their fins are fleshy and lobed rather than spiny. The fish belonging to this subclass are thought to be ancestors of modern amphibians.

Chondricthyes – this class of fish is made up of jawed fish having paired fins and skeletons made of cartilage rather than bone. The Chondricthyes class can be further divided into two subclasses: Elasmobranchii and Holocephali. The Elasmobranchii subclass contains sharks, rays and skates while the Holocephali group contains chimaeras, or ghost sharks. Members of the subclass Elasmobranchii have no swim bladders and they have an unfused jaw. The order Chimaeriformes is the only surviving group in the subclass Holocephali and the species in this order are poorly understood by modern scientists.

Placodermi – this class of fish contains prehistoric armored fish (now extinct) that lived during the Silurian and Devonian periods. These fish were among the first jawed species and their heads were covered by articulated armored plates while the rest of the body was naked or scaled. Fish belonging to this group are thought to have been primarily bottom-dwellers in both freshwater and shallow marine environments. Common opinion suggests that this group of fishes went extinct due to competition with the first bony fish and prehistoric sharks.

Acanthodii – this class of fishes is often referred to by the name "spiny sharks" and all fishes in this group are now extinct. In body, fishes in this group resembled sharks but their outer layer of skin (epidermis) was covered by rhomboid scales, thus giving them a combination of features found in bony and cartilaginous fish.

2) Saltwater Fish Groups

There are hundreds of families of fish currently in existence and some are more common than others. There is no reason for you to know every single family of fish out there, but you may be interested to see how certain species are grouped by order. Below you will find a list of some of the largest marine fish orders as well as examples of the fish belonging to each group:

5: Angelfish (Pomacanthidae), order Perciformes

Marine Fish by Shape

Shape Type	Examples
Rajiformes	Rays
Orectolobiformes	Sharks
Carcharhiniformes	Catsharks, Swellsharks, Sandbar Shark
Lamniformes	Mackerel Sharks
Lophiformes	Frogfish, Toadfish
Batrachoidiformes	Toadfish
Elopiformes	Tarpons, Bonefish, Milkfish

Albuliformes	Bonefish
Gonorhynchiformes	Milkfish
Anguilliformes	Eels
Siluriformes	Catfish
Beloniformes	Halfbeaks, Needlefish, Flying Fish
Scorpaeniformes	Scorpionfish, Stonefish, Flatheads, Velvetfish
Cyprinodontiformes	Toothcarps
Perciformes	Groupers, Snookes, Flagtail Perches, Cardinalfish, Remoras, Snappers, Trevallies, Moonfish, Ponyfish, Croakers, Goatfish, Wrasses, Parrotfish, Dragonets, Blennies, Barracudas, Damselfish, Cichlids, Butterflyfish, Angelfish, Gobies, Dartfish, Rabbitfish, Surgeonfish, Cowfish, Boxfish, Triggerfish, Pufferfish, Tuna, Mackerel, Swordfish, Sailfish, Marlin, Halibut, Flounder, Sole
Synbranchiformes	Swamp-eels
Gasterosteriformes	Pipefish, Seahorses, Cornetfish, Seamoth, Trumpetfish
Beryciformes	Soldierfish, Pinecone-fish
Clupeiformes	Sardines, Herring, Anchovies, Ilisha shads

Atheriniformes	Priapus-fish, Silversides
Aulopiformes	Lizardfish, Cusk-eels, Mullets
Gadiformes	Cod
Ophidiformes	Cusk-eels, Pearlfish, Brotulas
Mugiliformes	Sole

3) Freshwater Fish Groups

Of the thousands of species of fish that exist on the earth, an estimated 41 per cent live in freshwater habitats. Freshwater fish exhibit some of the greatest species diversity on the planet due to specialised adaptations and morphology resulting from isolated habitats like lakes and ponds. Below you will find a list of some of the largest freshwater fish families as well as examples of species in each group:

6: Discus Fish (Symphosodon), order Percirformes

Common Freshwater Fish Groups

Order Name	Examples
Lepisosteiformes	Gars
Amiiformes	Bowfin
Hiodontiformes	Mooneye, Goldeye
Cypriniformes	Barbs, Carp, Danios, Goldfish, Loaches, Minnows, Rasboras
Characiformes	Characins, Pencilfish, Hatchetfish, Piranha, Tetras, Pacu
Gymnotiformes	Electric Eel, Knifefish
Siluriformes	Catfish
Salmoniformes	Salmon, Trout
Esociformes	Pike
Osmeriformes	Smelts, Galaxiids
Cyprinodontiformes	Livebearers, Killifish
Perciformes	Bass, Sunfish, Cichlids, Gobies, Gouramis, Perch, Wrasses, Bettas, Anabantids
Tetraodontiformes	Pufferfish
Atheriniformes	Rainbowfish, Silversides

Glossary

Abyssal Zone – the deepest oceanic zone; water in this zone is high in oxygen content and highly pressurized, but it is also very cold and low in nutrients.

Acanthodians – the first jawed fish, existing during the Silurian and Devonian periods.

Agnathan – the first vertebrates; jawless fish with rounded mouth parts for filter feeding or sucking.

Anguilliform – a type of swimming motion in which the fish creates a deep body wave; ex: eels, lampreys and lungfish.

Benthic Zone – the oceanic zone between the pelagic zone and the abyssal zone; does not include the deepest waters of the ocean, but it does include layers of sand, silt and dead organisms.

Bioaccumulation – the accumulation of substances in an organism.

Bony Fish – a group of fish that began to evolve during the mid to late Devonian period; all bony fish possess an organ called a swim bladder that enables them to float at any water level.

Cartilaginous Fish – a group of fishes with no true bone, possessing instead cartilage or calcified cartilage for internal support.

Carangiform – a type of swimming motion in which the fish uses body flexion and caudal fin propulsion, creating an S-like body shape; ex: tuna.

Caudal Fin – tail; the fin located on the posterior end of the fish, used for locomotion.

Chordate - animals that have a dorsally situated central nervous system, gill clefts and a notochord in some stage of development.

Chromatophore - the scientific name for the pigment-containing cells which reflect light to produce colour; six different types, each named for its colour.

Dermis – the lower layer of skin from which scales grow; composed of blood vessels, fibroblasts and collagen.

Devonian Period – a period in the history of the earth lasting bout 63 million years, beginning about 417 million years ago and ending with the start of the Carboniferous period 354 million years ago.

Ectothermic - body temperature is regulated by the temperature of their surrounding environment
Endemic – unique to a specific geographical location – not naturally found anywhere else.

Endoskeleton – an internal structure formed by bones that serves to support and protect the body and organs.

Epidermis – the outer layer of skin; composed of epithelial cells which are constantly shed and replaced by new cells.

Estuary - a body of water where a freshwater river or stream meets with an ocean.

Eutrophication - the term used to describe an ecosystem's response to the addition of either natural or artificial substances.

Exoskeleton – a stable outer shell often made of cartilage or scales (as opposed to an internal skeleton.)

Filiform – an eel-like body plan in fish.

Fry – the name given to newly hatched fish.

Fusiform – a body plan in which the fish is streamlined from nose to tail.

Gill Arches - the tissue which lies between five slit-like openings on either side of the fish's body.

Gills – the means through which fish breathe underwater; composed of blood vessels covered by a thin layer of epithelial cells which facilitate the process of gas exchange.

Gonads – the reproductive organs of fish.

Intertidal Zone - the outermost oceanic zone, located where the ocean meets the land.

Invasive Species – a non-native (or introduced) species that has adverse effects on the habitat it invades.

Labyrinth - a lung-like organ found in certain freshwater fish belonging to the suborder Anabantoidei; allows fish to breathe oxygen directly from the air at the surface of the water, rather than filtering it through their gills.

Laterally Compressed – a body type in fish; thin. (eg, cichlids)

Laterally Depressed – a body type in fish; flat (eg, stingrays and flatfish.)

Limnetic Zone – open water area of a pond or lake surrounded by the littoral zone

Littoral Zone – uppermost zone of a lake or pond surrounding the edges of the shoreline; generally warm and well lit by sunlight.

Livebearer – a group of fishes that produces live young rather than eggs.

Milt – another name for the sperm produced by male fishes.

Mouth-brooding – a type of breeding in which the female gathers the eggs (either before or after fertilization) into her mouth to protect them while they develop.

Neuromast – small hair cells located in the bottom of a pit along the lateral line of fish; function as sensory cells.

Notochord - a rod that extends the length of the body, for example, a spine – that provides structure and support during movement.

Osmoregulation - the regulation of the osmotic pressure in an organism's fluids to maintain homeostasis.

Ostraciform – a type of swimming motion in which the fish primarily uses the caudal fin for propulsion, leaving the rest of the body steady; ex: boxfish and trunkfish.

Otolith – the ears of a fish.

Overfishing - used in reference to the taking of wildlife from a body of water at a rate that is too high to sustain; overharvesting.

Oviviparous – a type of livebearing fish that retains the eggs inside the body of the female, but they develop independently without receiving a supply of nutrients from the female's body.

Paraphyletic - all species in a single group diverged from a common ancestor.

Pelagic Zone – the second oceanic zone which includes the surface level of the open ocean.

Pharynx – another word for throat.

Placoderm – a group of heavily armored fish having a movable joint between the head and body; existed during the Silurian and Devonian periods.

Profundal Zone – deepest zone of a pond or lake; area largely unlit because light cannot penetrate the depths of the water.

Poikilothermic - the internal body temperature of an organism (like sharks) is the same as that of their environment.

Silurian Period - the period of time between about 443 and 417 million years ago.

Spawning - the process through which fish eggs are released and fertilised.

Swim Bladder - an internal organ though to have evolved from lungs which enables the fish to float at any water level.

Thermoregulation – the ability of an organism to maintain its body temperature despite a difference in the surrounding temperature.

Vermiform – a worm-like body plan in fish

Viviparous – a type of livebearing fish that provides nutrients to the eggs through the blood supply of the female (similar to the placenta in mammals.)

Weberian Ossicles – part of the Weberian Apparatus; a set of bones which connect the swim bladder to the auditory system, thus allowing the transmission of vibrations from the water around the fish into the inner ear.

Index

A

Australia · 57, 70, 71, 73, 74, 79, 88, 90, 170

B

bannerfish · 53, 55
barbell · 62, 86, 87
barbs · 53, 55, 61
barracuda · 55, 80, 81
barracudas · 44
bass · 8, 71, 80, 86, 92, 93, 116
basslet · 80, 99, 100
batfish · 53, 55
behaviour · 27, 28, 36, 37, 39, 41, 42, 43, 44, 160, 164, 176
benthic · 50, 51
Betta fish · 20
bioaccumulation · 112
biodiversity · 119
birth · 37, 38
Black Sea · 86
blood · 4, 15, 16, 17, 18, 26, 34, 38, 45, 135, 137, 140
bluefish · 92, 93, 99, 100
body plan · 12, 13, 29, 136, 140
body temperature · 23
bony · 4, 8, 13, 15, 19, 23, 43, 126, 127, 128, 134, 164
bottom-feeding · 6, 8
brackish · 45, 52
brain · 21
bream · 70, 78, 86, 87
breathe · 16, 20, 24, 26, 35, 137
breeding · 39, 83, 102, 123, 124, 138
butterflyfish · 55, 70, 73, 80, 81, 99, 100

C

camouflage · 41, 43
carangiform · 30
Carboniferous period · 5, 135
cardinalfish · 58, 71

D

E

H

M

Q

R

rainbowfish · 71
rasbora · 53, 104
ray-fin fish · 8
rays · 7, 8, 13, 21, 95, 127
Red Sea · 56, 57, 58, 60, 61, 63, 64, 66, 68, 69, 72, 73, 74, 76, 77, 78, 79, 82, 83, 85, 88, 89, 90, 91, 94, 96, 98, 101, 102, 103, 104, 105, 106, 108
reefs · 52, 75, 77, 80, 83, 114
remoras · 44
reproduction · 3, 2, 37, 160, 176
reproductive methods · 36
reptiles · 9
respiration · 21
rice paddies · 1, 20
Rift Lakes · 45
Rift Valley · 63
rivers · 47, 49, 60, 69, 78, 93, 111, 112, 113, 176
roach · 86
runoff · 111, 112

S

safety · 42
salmon · 8, 24, 26, 31, 86, 87
saltwater · 8, 22, 45, 49, 50, 52, 55, 63, 93, 127, 162
sand · 27, 51, 134
sawfish · 62
scales · 13, 15, 16, 34, 44, 72, 107, 128, 135, 136
schooling · 41, 42, 166
scorpionfish · 53
sea · 1, 5, 51, 91, 115, 116, 123, 124
SEA LIFE · 123, 124, 166
sensory systems · 11, 25, 176
shad · 92, 93
shape · 13, 27, 30, 31, 68, 71, 72, 73, 75, 101, 104, 135
sharks · 7, 8, 18, 21, 27, 44, 70, 126, 127, 128, 139

V

ventral fins · 14
vermiform · 12
vertebrates · 3, 4, 6, 8, 10, 12, 13, 17, 21, 22, 25, 34, 134, 176
vibrations · 20, 140
viviparous · 38

W

Weberian Apparatus · 19, 140
Western Hemisphere · 93
wetlands · 47, 110
whales · 51, 116
worm · 12, 140
wrasse · 70, 71, 77

Y

Yangtze River · 55

List of Relevant Websites
1) Fish Facts for Kids

United States Websites:

"All About Fish." The International Wildlife Rehabilitation Council

"Fun Fish Facts for Kids." Science Kids

"Fish." National Geographic

"All About Fish." Idaho Public Television

United Kingdom Websites:

"Fun Facts on Fish." Fun Facts for Kids. < Fun Facts
"Fish Facts." <http://www.thinkfish.co.uk/fun/fish-fact

"50 Fun Facts." http://www.national-aquarium.co.uk

"Fish and Kids." Marine Stewardship Council.
http://fishandkids.msc.org/

2) Evolutionary History of Fish

United States Websites:

Kagle, Rebecca. "The Evolutionary Steps of Fish.* Serendip Studio>

Maas, Daniel. "Fish Out of Water." ASU School of Life Sciences.
<http://askabiologist.asu.edu/plosable/fish-out-water>

"Evolution of Fish." Hooper Museum.
<http://hoopermuseum.earthsci.carleton.ca/coelacanth/F4.HTM>

"The Origin of Tetrapods." Understanding Evolution –Berkeley University of California.
<http://evolution.berkeley.edu/evolibrary/article/evograms_04>

United Kingdom Websites:

"History of Life on Earth." BBC Nature – Prehistoric Life. BBC - History of the Earth
Connor, Steve. "The 'Living Fossil' Coelacanth Fish Left Behind By Evolution." The Independent

"Ten Evolutionary Wonders of Fish." Practical Fish Keeping

"Aquarium Science – Evolution." Fish Tank and Ponds>

Singh, Kiran. "Hydrodynamics of Flexible Maneuvers in Fish." University of Cambridge - Department of Applied Mathematics and Theoretical Physics. http://people.maths.ox.ac.uk

"Fish Anatomical Terms." Fish Tanks and Ponds

"Osteichthyes – Characters and Anatomy." University of Bristol

United Kingdom Websites:

"Fish Reproduction and Development." TES Connect.
<http://www.tes.co.uk

Moe, Martin. "The Breeder's Net: Science, Biology and Terminology of Fish Reproduction." Advanced Aquarist. <http://www.advancedaquarist.com

"Fish Out of Water." BBC Weird Nature. <BBC
"Fish Reproductive Strategies." University of Edinburgh

3) Types and Species of Fish

United States Websites:

"The Classification of Fishes.". Earth Life

"A Picture Guide to Marine Fish Families." Habitat News

"Freshwater Fish Diversity." Freshwater Fish Specialist Group. http://www.iucnffsg.org

Berra, Tim. "Freshwater Fish Distribution Amazon.com

United Kingdom Websites:

"Shark and Skate Taxonomy." Shark Trust
"Fish Species Classification." British Sea Fishing

"Extinct Fish." University of Edinburgh>

"Fish Groups." Animal Corner

References

"Biology of Fishes." University of Washington.
<http://courses.washington.edu/fish311/FISH per cent20311 per cent20files/04-Locomotion.pdf>

Blundell, Adam. "Short Take: The Basics of Fish Locomotion."
Advanced Aquarist.
<http://www.advancedaquarist.com/2004/5/short>

"Bony Fishes – Behaviour." SeaWorld.org.
<http://seaworld.org/en/animal-info/animal-infobooks/bony-fish/behaviour/>

"Chordata." Animal Diversity Web.
<http://animaldiversity.ummz.umich.edu/accounts/Chordata/>

"Fish Sensory Systems." Minnesota Sea Grant.
<http://www.seagrant.umn.edu/fisheries/senses>

"Freshwater Threats." National Geographic.
<http://environment.nationalgeographic.com/environment/habitats/freshwater-threats/?rptregcta=reg_free_np&rptregcampaign=20131016_rw_membership_r1p_us_se_w#>

Hilber, Samantha A. "Mating Systems and Parental Care in Cichlids." Tropical Fish Hobbyist Magazine.
<http://www.tfhmagazine.com/details/articles/mating-systems-and-parental-care-in-cichlids.htm>

"History of Life on Earth." BBC Nature.
<http://www.bbc.co.uk/nature/history_of_the_earth>

"How do Fish Sleep?" Big Question. <https://bigquestion.wordpress.com/2008/03/04/how-do-fish-sleep/>

Kagle, Rebecca. "The Evolutionary Steps of Fish." Serendip Studio. <http://serendip.brynmawr.edu/exchange/node/1904>

Linendoll, Katie. "Lionfish Infestation in Atlantic Ocean a Growing Epidemic." CNN Tech. <http://www.cnn.com/2013/10/18/tech/innovation/lionfish-infestation-atlantic-linendoll/>

"Major Threats." The IUCN Red List of Threatened Species. <http://www.iucnredlist.org/initiatives/freshwater/panafrica/threats>

"Marine Habitat Destruction." National Geographic. <http://ocean.nationalgeographic.com/ocean/critical-issues-marine-habitat-destruction/>

Morfitt, Craig. "Lake Tanganyika and its Diverse Cichlids." Cichlid-Forum.com. < http://www.cichlid-forum.com/articles/lake_tanganyika_diverse.php>

"Overfishing." National Geographic. <http://ocean.nationalgeographic.com/ocean/critical-issues-overfishing/>

"Protect Our Seas." SEA LIFE London Aquarium. <http://www.visitsealife.com/london/protect-our-seas/>

Ramel, Gordon. "Locomotion in Fish." Earthlife.net.
<http://www.earthlife.net/fish/locomotion.html>

Reebs, Stephan G. "Aggression in Fishes." How Fish Behave.
<http://www.howfishbehave.ca/pdf/
aggression.pdf>
Stout, Prentice K. "Fish Schooling." Rhode Island Sea Grant Fact
Sheet. <http://seagrant.gso.uri.edu/factsheets/
schooling.html>

"The Aquatic Biome." The University of California Museum of
Paleontology.
<http://www.ucmp.berkeley.edu/glossary/gloss5/biome/aquatic.
html>

Turner, S.J., et al. "Fishing Impacts and the Degradation or Loss
of Habitat Structure." *The Journal of Fisheries Management and
Ecology*, 1999, 6, 401-420.
<http://globalrestorationnetwork.org/uploads/files/LiteratureAtta
chments/149_fishing-impacts-and-the-degradation-or-loss-of-
habitat-structure.pdf>

Wilkins, Sabine. "The Evolution of Cichlids." Cichlid-
Forum.com. < http://www.cichlid-forum.com/articles/
evol_cich_pt1.php>

Photo Credits

Astraspis desiderata by Philippe Janvier via Wikimedia Commons, <http://en.wikipedia.org/wiki/File:Astraspis_desiderata.gif>

Coelacanth, By Alberto Fernandez via Wikimedia Commons, <http://en.wikipedia.org/wiki/File:Latimeria_Chalumnae_-_Coelacanth_-_NHMW.jpg>

Directions, By Esseh via Wikimedia Commons, <http://en.wikipedia.org/wiki/File:Anatomical_Directions_and_Axes.JPG>

Anatomy, By Sharon High School via Wikimedia Commons, <http://en.wikipedia.org/wiki/File:Internal_organs_of_a_fish.jpg>

Osmoregulation, By Kare via Wikimedia Commons, <http://en.wikipedia.org/wiki/File:Osmoseragulation_Carangoides_bartholomaei_bw_en2.png>

Flying Fish, By Haplochromis via Wikimedia Commons, <http://en.wikipedia.org/wiki/File:Pink-wing_flying_fish.jpg>

Lake Tanganyika, By NASA via Wikimedia Commons, <http://en.wikipedia.org/wiki/File:STS51G-034-0012_Lake_Tanganyika_June1985.jpg>

Oceanic Zones, By Chris Huh via Wikimedia Commons, <http://en.wikipedia.org/wiki/File:Oceanic_divisions.svg>

World Map, By Benji2 via Wikimedia Commons, <http://commons.wikimedia.org/wiki/File:Worldmap_LandAndPolitical.jpg>

Tilapia, By Bjorn Christian Torressen via Wikimedia Commons, <http://en.wikipedia.org/wiki/File:Oreochromis-niloticus-Nairobi.JPG>

Australia Map, By Central Intelligence Agency [Public domain], via Wikimedia Commons, <http://commons.wikimedia.org/wiki/File: per cent22Political_Oceania per cent22_CIA_World_Factbook.jpg>

Tang, By Tewy via Wikimedia Commons, <http://en.wikipedia.org/wiki/File:Blue_tang_(Paracanthurus_he patus)_02.jpg>

Butterflyfish, By Leonard Low from Australia via Wikimedia Commons, <http://en.wikipedia.org/wiki/File:Chaetodon_ephippium_PLW_edit.jpg>

Clownfish, By Metatron via Wikimedia Commons, <http://en.wikipedia.org/wiki/File:Ocellaris_clownfish.JPG>

Angelfish, By Jacek Madejski via Wikimedia Commons, <http://en.wikipedia.org/wiki/File:Pygoplites_diacanthus_by_Jac ek_Madejski.jpg>

Wrasse, By Lonnie Huffman via Wikimedia Commons, <http://en.wikipedia.org/wiki/File:Six-line_wrasse.jpg>

Bream, By Lvova via Wikimedia Commons, <http://en.wikipedia.org/wiki/File:Carp_bream1.jpg>

Cod, By Fir0002 via Wikimedia Commons, <http://en.wikipedia.org/wiki/File:Murray_cod02_melb_aquariu m.jpg>

Caribbean Map, By Kmusser (Own work, all data from Vector Map.) [CC-BY-SA-3.0 (http://creativecommons.org/licenses/by-sa/3.0)], via Wikimedia Commons, <http://commons.wikimedia.org/wiki/File:Caribbean_general_map.png>

Lionfish, By Alexandar Vasenin via Wikimedia Commons, <http://en.wikipedia.org/wiki/File:Red_lionfish_near_Gilli_Banta_Island.JPG>

Damselfish, By USGS via Wikimedia Commons, <http://en.wikipedia.org/wiki/File:Cocoa_damselfish.jpg>

Goatfish, By Hectonichus via Wikimedia Commons, <http://en.wikipedia.org/wiki/File:Mullidae_-_Mulloidichthys_vanicolensis.jpg>

Perch, via Wikimedia Commons, <http://commons.wikimedia.org/wiki/File:Russian_River_tule_perch.jpg>

Brown Trout, via Wikimedia Commons, <http://commons.wikimedia.org/wiki/File:Brown_trout.JPG>

Page 89, Europe Map, By lib.utexas.edu states The following maps were produced by the U.S. Central Intelligence Agency, unless otherwise indicated. (http://www.lib.utexas.edu/maps/europe.html) [Public domain], via Wikimedia Commons, <http://commons.wikimedia.org/wiki/File:2008_Europe_Political_Map_EN.jpg>

Dogfish, By NOAA via Wikimedia Commons, <http://en.wikipedia.org/wiki/File:Spiny_dogfish.jpg>

Flounder, By Hectonichus via Wikimedia Commons, <http://en.wikipedia.org/wiki/File:Bothidae_-_Bothus_mancus.jpg>

Perch, By Citron via Wikimedia Commons, <http://en.wikipedia.org/wiki/File:Perca_fluviatilis2.jpg>

Trout, By Eric Engbretson for U.S. Fish and Wildlife Service [Public domain], via Wikimedia Commons, <http://commons.wikimedia.org/wiki/File:Salmo_trutta.jpg>

Haddock, via Wikimedia Commons, <http://commons.wikimedia.org/wiki/File:Haddock,_Boston_Aquarium.JPG>

Pupfish, via Wikimedia Commons, <http://commons.wikimedia.org/wiki/File:Comanche_Springs_pupfish.jpg>

North America Map, By Central Intelligence Agency [Public domain], via Wikimedia Commons, <http://commons.wikimedia.org/wiki/File:Map_North_America.PNG>

Snapper, By NOAA Fish Watch via Wikimedia Commons, <http://en.wikipedia.org/wiki/File:Red_snapper_2.jpg>

Goby, By Brian Gratwicke via Wikimedia Commons, <http://en.wikipedia.org/wiki/File:Rhinogobiops_nicholsii;_Black eye_goby.jpg>

Catfish, By Citron via Wikimedia Commons, <http://en.wikipedia.org/wiki/File:Catfishh.jpg>

CPSIA information can be obtained
at www.ICGtesting.com
Printed in the USA
BVHW062034210620
581982BV00001B/11